Your Personal
Horoscope
2019

♑

Capricorn

YOUR PERSONAL HOROSCOPE 2019

CAPRICORN

22nd December–20th January

igloobooks

igloobooks

Published in 2018
by Igloo Books Ltd
Cottage Farm
Sywell
NN6 0BJ
www.igloobooks.com

Produced for Igloo Books Ltd by Foulsham Publishing Ltd, The Old Barrel Store,
Drayman's Lane, Marlow, Bucks SL7 2FF, England

FIR003 0718
2 4 6 8 10 9 7 5 3 1
ISBN: 978-1-78810-500-2

This is an abridged version of material originally published
in Old Moore's Horoscope and Astral Diary.

Cover designed by Nicholas Gage
Edited by Bobby Newlyn-Jones

Printed and manufactured in China

CONTENTS

CONTENTS

INTRODUCTION

Your personal horoscopes have been specifically created to allow you to get the most from astrological patterns and the way they have a bearing on not only your zodiac sign, but nuances within it. Using the diary section of the book you can read about the influences and possibilities of each and every day of the year. It will be possible for you to see when you are likely to be cheerful and happy or those times when your nature is in retreat and you will be more circumspect. The diary will help to give you a feel for the specific 'cycles' of astrology and the way they can subtly change your day-to-day life. For example, when you see the sign ☿, this means that the planet Mercury is retrograde at that time. Retrograde means it appears to be running backwards through the zodiac. Such a happening has a significant effect on communication skills, but this is only one small aspect of how the personal horoscope can help you.

With your personal horoscope the story doesn't end with the diary pages. It includes simple ways for you to work out the zodiac sign the Moon occupied at the time of your birth, and what this means for your personality. In addition, if you know the time of day you were born, it is possible to discover your Ascendant, yet another important guide to your personal make-up and potential.

Many readers are interested in relationships and in knowing how well they get on with people of other astrological signs. You might also be interested in the way you appear to very different sorts of individuals. If you are such a person, the section on Venus will be of particular interest. Despite the rapidly changing position of this planet, you can work out your Venus sign, and learn what bearing it will have on your life.

Using your personal horoscope you can travel on one of the most fascinating and rewarding journeys that anyone can take – the journey to a better realisation of self.

THE ESSENCE OF CAPRICORN

Exploring the Personality of Capricorn the Goat

(22ND DECEMBER – 20TH JANUARY)

What's in a sign?

You probably think of yourself as being the least complicated person to be found anywhere. Although this is basically true, that doesn't necessarily mean that everyone understands you quite as well as they might. When faced with the real world you are practical, capable and resourceful. That means that you get on well with whatever needs to be done. Where you might sometimes fall down is in terms of communicating your intentions to the world at large – mostly it doesn't seem all that important to do so. In other words, you are not the world's best talker, and probably don't even want to be.

When it comes to sweeping away the red tape and actually getting down to the task in hand, you are second to none. Dextrous and adaptable in all matters that need your unique logic, you come at all problems with the same determination to sort them out. However, your ruling planet is cold, ponderous Saturn, and that could be where the potential problems start. Although you have a kind heart and a genuine desire to improve the lot of others, your methods are sometimes misunderstood. Some people might think you a little aloof, or even difficult to talk to. You have frequent quiet spells and often seem to be particularly content with your own company. On rare occasions this can leave you isolated.

Sharing what you are with the world at large is the most important factor on the road to a more contented life, though even this isn't certain, because most Capricorn people tend to be fairly happy with being the way they are. All the same, when those around you want to see something actually being done, they will call on you. Success is not hard for you to achieve, particularly in a career sense. You don't mind getting your hands dirty and can usually be relied upon to find ingenious answers when they are most needed.

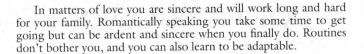

   In matters of love you are sincere and will work long and hard for your family. Romantically speaking you take some time to get going but can be ardent and sincere when you finally do. Routines don't bother you, and you can also learn to be adaptable.

Capricorn resources

You probably don't think of yourself as being the most dynamic person in the world, though you certainly are one of the most capable. When others are looking for answers, even in very practical matters, you are in there sorting things out. It's the nuts and bolts of the world that are most important, and you don't seem to have too much trouble fixing broken things – whether it's the living room chair, or the heart of a dear friend.

   Instead of trying to be one of life's exciting go-getters, you are likely to be more comfortable working slowly and steadily, sometimes in the background. But this doesn't mean that you fail to make a positive impression. On the contrary, you are very necessary to those who form a part of your life, and they are ever aware of the important part you play. It isn't given to everyone to be showy and flashy, and in any case even if you forced yourself down such roads you probably wouldn't be at all comfortable in a role that doesn't come naturally to you.

   One of your greatest attributes is your dry sense of humour. It's always possible for you to make others laugh, even during the most awkward or difficult situations. When the world looks particularly dark we all need a Capricorn subject along to lighten the load. You make a good colleague, know well how to co-operate and tend to work capably, either as part of a team, or when circumstances dictate, on your own.

   Your greatest resource, and the one that has made many Capricorn people famous over the years, is your capacity to keep going. When there is a problem to be solved, a bridge to build, or a family to support under difficult circumstances, you really come into your own. This is probably because you don't understand the meaning of the word failure. You can find ways round any number of obstacles, and remain dependable, even when the world and his dog are falling to pieces. Add to this the fact that you are consistent and reliable and it shouldn't be too hard for you to enjoy being a capable Capricorn.

Beneath the surface

Although you might not appear to be very complicated when viewed from the perspective of those who see you on a daily basis, you are actually very complex. The reason that this is not obvious lies in the fact that you betray very little of your inner mind in your day-to-day interactions with others. In the main they see you as being capable and settled – but how wrong they can be.

The fact is that you are rarely totally sure of yourself. The confidence to get things done disguises how often you shake inside, and especially so if you are forced into the public arena. You probably wouldn't relish having to do any sort of presentation or to be put on the spot in front of individuals you consider to be more dynamic than you are. Despite this there are strong saving graces. Even when times are tough, or when you do feel a little shaky inside, your natural way forward is to keep plugging away. In some respects your zodiac sign may represent one of the bravest of them all. You won't allow yourself to be bettered by anyone, and the more pressure that is put upon you to fail, the greater is your internal desire for success.

In matters of emotion you are complicated and difficult to understand. You view relationships with the same patience that you bring to almost all facets of life. Friends can misuse or even abuse you for a while, but there is a breaking point within Capricorn that appears sudden, and very final. And once you have made up your mind to a particular course of action, there isn't any force in the world that will prevent you from implementing it.

Your natural planetary ruler is Saturn, the Lord of Time. As a result you are inclined to see things in the medium and longer term. You rarely show yourself to be impatient and carefully choose a course of action, using mental processes that usually follow tried and tested paths. You won't be hurried or pushed and will always stick to methods of working that seem to have worked for you in the past. Although this might sometimes make you feel lacking in colour or variety, you almost always get where you want to go. Occasionally your inner mind takes a great leap in logic. This can lead to a sudden change in attitude and actions that will shock the world. And why not? Even Capricorns need to keep people guessing sometimes.

You may not be the easiest person in the world to understand, or to get to know fully. Don't worry. The inner secrecy of your nature is half your appeal.

Making the best of yourself

We all need to realise what makes us tick, and to come to terms with the most comfortable way in which we can react with the world at large. This is just as true for the zodiac sign of Capricorn as it is for any other. But nobody is perfect, so what can you do to use your skills to the full and to get on better with those who share the planet with you?

Well for starters, it wouldn't be a bad idea to let others know what you are doing – and why. In practical situations especially it's sometimes much easier for you simply to get on and finish a task on your own. And despite your capabilities this is probably why you are not the world's best teacher. It's simply less complicated to get something done, and then to move on patiently to the next demand. On the way, however, you might alienate those who would love to be your friends, and to learn from you.

When it comes to emotion you should do your best to explain the way you feel. Building up animosity for days, weeks or even months, doesn't really do anyone a lot of good, not even a Capricorn subject. People can't alter to suit your needs if they don't know what it is you want. For this reason you should always be as honest as you can be, even if this proves to be quite embarrassing at first. Be willing to show your flexible side – and even to create one if necessary. Try doing things the way others want to proceed now and again, despite the fact that you could be convinced that they are wrong in their approach. Allowing those around you the right to fail is important and in the end it will only make you look that much more confident and together when you stoop to pick up the pieces.

As often as proves to be possible you should display the inner smile that burns away inside you. Be willing to let your hair down and have a good time in the company of people who really do want to know that you are happy. Most important of all, share your inner honesty with those who are important to you.

The impressions you give

There is a great disparity between the way you feel about certain situations, and the impression you offer to an unsuspecting world. If you could fully see yourself as others usually see you, it's an odds-on certainty that you would be very surprised. The vast majority of those with whom you live and work see you as being ultra confident, very cool and quite capable. If you find this hard to believe, simply ask the most honest of your friends. It doesn't matter how you feel inside, or that you often have to dig around for answers that don't supply themselves immediately. What counts is the barrier that is placed constantly between your inner mind and your outward persona.

This is very important because it means you could get on in life even better than you may appear to be doing at the moment. Think what a great gift it is rarely to show that you are quaking inside. And when your cool approach means that you find advancement coming your way, you move on to the next set of requirements with the same apparent confidence you had before.

On a less positive note, it is possible that certain of the people with whom you interact on a daily basis could find you somewhat cold and even perhaps a little aloof on occasions. This is not the case, but once again there is a screen between the way you feel and the façade you show to the world at large. And though this barrier can be your best friend, it can also be a powerful enemy, especially in emotional or romantic situations. When circumstances necessitate, it is important that you tell those with whom you share your life exactly how you feel. That allows them to modify their own behaviour to suit your needs.

There may not be a great deal of work to do on altering your approach because in the main you are well liked and certainly respected. All that is really required in any case is an understanding that what you think and the way you act are not necessarily the same thing.

The way forward

Although it's true of course that anyone can make favourable alterations to their life, it's entirely possible that yours is already headed in the right direction generally. Capricorn people are not usually too complicated; they remain modest in their objectives and can achieve their ends through the medium of good ideas and hard work. You may not give the impression of being the most exciting person in the world – and nor do you wish to be. But when it's necessary to come up with the goods, mentally and practically, you don't usually have much trouble doing so.

To be and to remain quietly confident isn't too much to ask from life. Under most circumstances you take on tasks that you know you can achieve, try to be kind to others on the way and don't tend to make too many waves. It probably doesn't bother you too much that there are people around who may not care for you. This is essentially because you are a realist and understand that you won't be everyone's cup of tea.

If there are points within your nature that could be improved with effort they might relate to a certain stubborn streak. There are occasions when you become very determined to achieve a particular objective and you may not always listen to alternatives once you think you know how to proceed. However, since you don't tend to take on tasks that you are not equipped to deal with, what some may call intransigence, you might refer to as self-assurance. It is also possible that you sometimes find it difficult to express your inner feelings, and especially those related to love. You can be somewhat suspicious of the motives of others and may guard yourself a little too carefully as a result.

Try to recognise that there is more than one way to skin a cat, and that you can actually learn and grow through co-operation. You may also need to be willing to take on a greater degree of responsibility at work, even though this might go against the grain for a whole host of reasons. When faced with decisions that have a bearing on the lives of others, seek their counsel and take note of their opinions.

There are times when you can be a little too pessimistic for your own good. It is important to cultivate a cheerful approach, even though your sometimes slightly gloomy attitude is actually revered and smiled at by your friends. You are loyal, hard-working and generally kind. Capricorn may not be the most dynamic of the zodiac signs, but it is hard to fault it all the same.

CAPRICORN ON THE CUSP

Astrological profiles are altered for those people born at either the beginning or the end of a zodiac sign, or, more properly, on the cusps of a sign. In the case of Capricorn this would be on the 22nd of December and for two or three days after, and similarly at the end of the sign, probably from the 18th to the 20th of January.

The Sagittarius Cusp – 22nd December to 24th December

Oh, what a lovely person you can be, and how respected you are by the world at large. At its best this is a very fortunate combination because it retains all the practical skills of Capricorn, but the nature is somewhat elevated by the quality of Sagittarius. Nothing much is beyond your capabilities but, unlike the typical Sagittarian, you back up your words with some quite practical actions. People learn to trust you and the amount of reliance that is placed on your judgement is sometimes staggering. Of course this does infer a high degree of responsibility but this fact probably won't worry you in the slightest. From a personal point of view you are very good to know and do your best to be friendly to almost everyone. However, you don't suffer fools at all gladly and probably prefer the company of those whose thoughts and ideas run along the same sort of road as yours.

Nobody could dispute the fact that you are very reasonable but you do sometimes get so obsessed with things that you could be less accessible than Sagittarius. A little extra work may be needed in this direction, especially when you are dealing with people who don't have your fast-track approach to problems. For all this you are a deep thinker and will often weigh up the pros and cons of a particular problem if necessary. In love you are deep and sincere, but with a superficial veneer that makes you appear light, bright and fun to be with. Making your way in life isn't at all difficult and money could easily come your way. This is not a response to good luck, but to dedication and inspired hard work.

With a good combination of the practical and the inspirational, you could turn your hand to almost anything. Your confidence is usually high and you are always in a good position to get by, no matter what obstacles you encounter. You like a challenge and rarely shy away from things when the going gets tough. This is one of the reasons that others like you so much and also explains why they have such confidence in your abilities. Your sense of purpose is strong and you may be tougher than you realise.

The Aquarius Cusp – 18th January to 20th January

This is the more dreamy side of Capricorn and can make for an individual who is sometimes rather difficult for others to fathom. This is hardly surprising since you don't really know your own nature quite as well as you would wish. Because the two zodiac signs are a little like oil and water you can rub along quite nicely for ages as a typical Capricorn, before suddenly shooting off at a tangent into some nether world that isn't at all like the reliable sign of the Goat. You tend to think about things fairly deeply, though with a rather 'off the wall' approach that sometimes annoys your deeper Capricorn traits. Certainly you are fascinating to know, with a magnetic personality and a basic charm that shows itself a great deal, especially when your interest is roused.

You are a lover of mystery and might appear on occasion to have a slightly dark side. This is really only a sort of morbid curiosity and it doesn't reflect your own basic nature, which is kind, sincere and anxious to please. Socially you contribute to anything that takes your fancy but you won't stay around long if you find a conversation boring. Finding the right sort of romantic partner might be somewhat difficult because you are not run-of-the-mill and have strange needs at a personal level. However, once you have set your sights in a particular direction, you stick to it. And as far as finding the right person is concerned, you could do much worse than to trust your intuition, which is strong. You don't always know what you want from life, but this fact can prove to be half of the fascination.

This unusual nature tends to fit you for occupations that demand a variety of skills, though you may change your career entirely at some stage in your life. Certainly you can be very practical, but the way things feel is important to you and you might find that you start certain tasks time and again in order to make sure that they turn out just right. This sign combination can easily lead to a desire for travel and a need to extend your personal horizons. Your restlessness is sometimes a puzzle to others, but it's a fascination, too.

CAPRICORN AND ITS ASCENDANTS

The nature of every individual on the planet is composed of the rich variety of zodiac signs and planetary positions that were present at the time of their birth. Your Sun sign, which in your case is Capricorn, is one of the many factors when it comes to assessing the unique person you are. Probably the most important consideration, other than your Sun sign, is to establish the zodiac sign that was rising over the eastern horizon at the time that you were born. This is your Ascending or Rising sign. Most popular astrology fails to take account of the Ascendant, and yet its importance remains with you from the very moment of your birth, through every day of your life. The Ascendant is evident in the way you approach the world, and so, when meeting a person for the first time, it is this astrological influence that you are most likely to notice first. Our Ascending sign essentially represents what we appear to be, while the Sun sign is what we feel inside ourselves.

The Ascendant also has the potential for modifying our overall nature. For example, if you were born at a time of day when Capricorn was passing over the eastern horizon (this would be around the time of dawn) then you would be classed as a double Capricorn. As such, you would typify this zodiac sign, both internally and in your dealings with others. However, if your Ascendant sign turned out to be an Air sign, such as Gemini, there would be a profound alteration of nature, away from the expected qualities of Capricorn.

One of the reasons why popular astrology often ignores the Ascendant is that it has always been rather difficult to establish. We have found a way to make this possible by devising an easy-to-use table, which you will find on page 157 of this book. Using this, you can establish your Ascendant sign at a glance. You will need to know your rough time of birth, then it is simply a case of following the instructions.

For those readers who have no idea of their time of birth it might be worth allowing a good friend, or perhaps your partner, to read through the section that follows this introduction. Someone who deals with you on a regular basis may easily discover your Ascending sign, even though you could have some difficulty establishing it for yourself. A good understanding of this component of your nature is essential if you want to be aware of that 'other person' who is responsible for the way you make contact with the world at large. Your Sun sign, Ascendant sign, and the other pointers in this book will, together, allow you a far better understanding of what makes you tick as an individual. Peeling back the different layers of your astrological make-up can be an enlightening experience, and the Ascendant may represent one of the most important layers of all.

Capricorn with Capricorn Ascendant

Whatever it is that you are looking for in life, there isn't much doubt that you find it. Having done so, you tend to consolidate your position before looking ahead to the next set of objectives. There isn't a more determined soul than you in the length and breadth of the whole zodiac and you will not be thwarted once you have made up your mind. It would take an astute person to pull the wool over your eyes in any practical respect, though you may not be quite so clever when it comes to the personal side of your life. You can sometimes be rather misled in love, but not if you are as determined in this direction as you are in every other sphere of life.

The most enduring quality that you possess is staying-power, and you remain certain that your long-term plans are the right ones, modifying here and tweaking there to get them just right. On the way you make few deep friends, though the ones you do have tend to stay around for years. All the same you are popular, and can attract the right sort of people to help you out. In love you are sincere and honest, a good and reliable partner, and, supposedly, one of the best lovers to be found in a month of Sundays. All you need to complete the picture is a more flexible attitude.

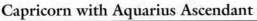

Capricorn with Aquarius Ascendant

Here the determination of Capricorn is assisted by a slightly more adaptable quality and an off-beat personality that tends to keep everyone else guessing. You don't care to be quite so predictable as the archetypal Capricorn would be and there is a more idealistic quality, or at least one that shows more. A greater number of friends than Capricorn would usually keep is likely, though less than a true Aquarian would gather. Few people doubt your sincerity, though not all of them understand what makes you tick. Unfortunately you are not in a position to help them out, because you are not very sure yourself. All the same you muddle through and can be very capable when the mood takes you.

Being a natural traveller, you love to see new places and would be quite fascinated by cultures that are very different to your own. People with this combination are inclined to spend some time living abroad and may even settle there. You look out for the underdog and will always have time for a good cause, no matter what it takes to help. In romantic terms you are a reliable partner, though with a slightly wayward edge which, if anything, tends to make you more attractive. Listen to your intuition, which rarely lets you down. Generally speaking you are very popular.

Capricorn with Pisces Ascendant

You are certainly not the easiest person in the world to understand, mainly because your nature is so deep and your personality so complicated, that others are somewhat intimidated at the prospect of staring into this abyss. All the same your friendly nature is attractive, and there will always be people around who are fascinated by the sheer magnetic quality that is endemic to the zodiac mix. Sentimental and extremely kind, there is no limit to the extent of your efforts on behalf of a deserving world, though there are some people around who wonder at your commitment and who may ridicule you a little for your staying-power, even in the face of some adversity. At work you are very capable, will work long and hard, and can definitely expect a greater degree of financial and practical success than Pisces alone. Routines don't bother you too much, though you do need regular periods of introspection, which help to recharge low batteries and a battered self-esteem.

In affairs of the heart you are somewhat given to impulse, which belies the more careful qualities of Capricorn. However, the determination remains intact and you are quite capable of chasing rainbows around, never realising that you can't get to the end of them. You are immensely lovable and a great favourite to many.

Capricorn with Aries Ascendant

If ever anyone could be accused of setting off immediately, but slowly, it has to be you. These are very contradictory signs and the differences will express themselves in a variety of ways. One thing is certain, you have tremendous tenacity and will see a job through patiently from beginning to end, without tiring on the way, and ensuring that every detail is taken care of properly. This combination often bestows good health and a great capacity for continuity, particularly in terms of the length of life. You are certainly not as argumentative as the typical Aries, but you do know how to get your own way, which is just as well because you are usually thinking on behalf of everyone else and not just on your own account.

At home you can relax, which is a blessing for Aries, though in fact you seldom choose to do so because you always have some project or other on the go. You probably enjoy knocking down and rebuilding walls, though this is a practical tendency and not responsive to relationships, in which you are ardent and sincere. Impetuosity is as close to your heart as is the case for any type of Aries subject, though you certainly have the ability to appear patient and steady. But it's really just a front, isn't it?

Capricorn with Taurus Ascendant

It might appear on the surface that you are not the most interesting person in the world. This is a pity, for you have an active though very logical mind, so logical in some instances that you would have a great deal in common with Mr Spock. This is the thorn in your flesh, or rather the flesh of everyone else, since you are probably quite happy being exactly what you are. You can think things through in a clear and very practical way and end up taking decisions that are balanced, eminently sensible, but, on occasions, rather dull.

Actually there is a fun machine somewhere deep within that Earth-sign nature and those who know you the best will recognise the fact. Often this combination is attended by a deep and biting sense of humour, but it's of the sort that less intelligent and considered types would find rather difficult to recognise. It is likely that you have no lack of confidence in your own judgement, and you have all the attributes necessary to do very well on the financial front. Slow and steady progress is your way and you need to be quite certain before you commit yourself to any new venture. This is a zodiac combination that can soak up years of stress and numerous difficulties and yet still come out on top. Nothing holds you back for long and you tend to be very brave.

Capricorn with Gemini Ascendant

A very careful and considered combination is evident here. You still have the friendly and chatty qualities of Gemini, though you also possess an astute, clever and deep-thinking quality which can really add bite to the Mercurial aspects of your nature. Although you rarely seem to take yourself or anyone else too seriously, in reality you are not easily fooled and usually know the direction in which you are heading. The practical application of your thought processes matter to you and you always give of your best, especially in any professional situation. This combination provides the very best business mind that any Gemini could have and, unlike other versions of the sign, you are willing to allow matters to mature. This quality cannot be overstated and leads to a form of ultimate achievement that many other Geminis would only guess at.

Family matters are important to you and your home is a special place of retreat, even though you are also willing to get out and meet the world, which is the prerogative of all Gemini types. There are times when you genuinely wish to remain quiet, and when such times arise you may need to explain the situation to some of the bemused people surrounding you. Above all you look towards material gain, though without ever losing your sense of humour.

Capricorn with Cancer Ascendant

The single most important factor here is the practical ability to get things done and to see any task, professional or personal, through to the end. Since half this combination is Cancer that also means expounding much of your energy on behalf of others. There isn't a charity in the world that would fail to recognise what a potent combination this is when it comes to the very concrete side of offering help and assistance. Many of your ideas hold water and you don't set off on abortive journeys of any kind, simply because you tend to get the ground rules fixed in your mind first.

On a more personal level you can be rather hard to get to know, because both these signs have a deep quality and a tendency to keep things in the dark. The mystery may only serve to encourage people to try and get to know you better. As a result you could attract a host of admirers, many of whom would wish to form romantic attachments. This may prove to be irrelevant however, because once you give your heart, you tend to be loyal and would only change your mind if you were pushed into doing so. Prolonged periods of inactivity don't do you any good and it is sensible for you to keep on the move, even though your progress in life is measured and very steady.

Capricorn with Leo Ascendant

What really sets you apart is your endless patience and your determination to get where you want to go, no matter how long it takes you to do so. On the way there are many sub-plots in your life and a wealth of entertaining situations to keep you amused. Probably somewhat quieter than the average Leo, you still have the capacity to be the life and soul of the party on those occasions when it suits you to be so. Energy, when allied to persistence, is a powerful commodity and you have a great need to take on causes of one sort or another. Probably at your best when defending the rights of the oppressed, you take the protecting qualities of Leo to greater heights than almost anyone else touched by the idealistic and regal qualities of the sign. If arguments come into your life, you deal with them quickly and, in the main, wisely. Like most Capricorn types you take to a few individuals, who will play a part in your life for years on end.

Being a good family type, your partner and children are very important and you will lavish the same patience, determination and ultimate success on their behalf that you do when dealing with more remote situations. The fact is that you do not know any other way to behave, and you are at your best when there is a mountain to climb.

Capricorn with Virgo Ascendant

Your endurance, persistence and concentration are legendary, and there is virtually nothing that eludes you once you have the bit between your teeth. You are not the pushy, fussy, go-getting sort of Virgoan but are steady, methodical and very careful. Once you have made up your mind, a whole team of wild horses could not change it, and although this can be a distinct blessing at times, it is a quality that can bring odd problems into your life too. The difficulty starts when you adopt a lost or less than sensible cause. Even in the face of overwhelming negative evidence, there is something inside you that prevents any sort of U-turn and so you carry on as solidly as only you can, to a destination that won't suit you at all.

There are few people around who are more loyal and constant than you can be. There is a lighter and brighter side to your nature, and the one or two people who are most important in your life will know how to bring it out. You have a wicked sense of humour, particularly if you have had a drink or when you are feeling on top form. Travel does you the world of good, even if there is a part of you that would rather stay at home. You have a potent, powerful and magnetic personality, but for much of the time it is kept carefully hidden.

Capricorn with Libra Ascendant

It is a fact that Libra is the most patient of the Air signs, though like the others it needs to get things done fairly quickly. Capricorn, on the other hand, will work long and hard to achieve its objectives and will not be thwarted. As a result this is a powerful combination and one that leads ultimately to success.

Capricorn is often accused of taking itself too seriously, and yet it has an ironic and really very funny sense of humour which only its chief confidants recognise. Libra is lighthearted, always willing to have fun and quite anxious to please. When these two basic types come together in their best forms, you might find yourself to be one of the most well- balanced people around. Certainly you know what you want, but don't have to use a bulldozer in order to get it.

Active and enthusiastic when something really takes your fancy, you might also turn out to be one of the very best lovers of them all. The reason for this is that you have the depth of Capricorn but the lighter and more directly affectionate qualities of the Scales. What you want from life in a personal sense, you eventually tend to get, but you don't care too much if this takes you a while. Few people could deny that you are a faithful friend, a happy sort and a deeply magnetic personality.

Capricorn with Scorpio Ascendant

If patience, perseverance and a solid ability to get where you want to go are considered to be the chief components of a happy life, then you should be skipping about every day. Unfortunately this is not always the case, and here we have two zodiac signs who can both be too deep for their own good. Both Scorpio and Capricorn are inclined to take themselves rather too seriously, and your main lesson in life, and some would say the reason you have adopted this zodiac combination, is to 'lighten up'. If all that determination is pushed in the direction of your service to the world at large, you are seen as being one of the kindest people imaginable. This is really the only option for you, because if you turn this tremendous potential power inwards all the time you will become brooding, secretive and sometimes even selfish. Your eyes should be turned towards a needy humanity, which can be served with the dry but definite wit of Capricorn and the true compassion of Scorpio.

It is impossible with this combination to indicate what areas of life suit you the best. Certainly you adore luxury in all its forms, and yet you can get by with almost nothing. You desire travel, and at the same time love the comforts and stability of home. The people who know you best are aware that you are rather special. Listen to what they say.

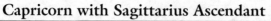

Capricorn with Sagittarius Ascendant

The typical Sagittarian nature is modified for the better when Capricorn is part of the deal. It's true that you manage to push forward progressively under most circumstances, but you also possess staying power and can work long and hard to achieve your objectives, most of which are carefully planned in advance. Few people have the true measure of your nature, for it runs rather deeper than appears to be the case on the surface. Routines don't bother you as much as would be the case for Sagittarius when taken alone, and you don't care if any objective takes weeks, months or even years to achieve. You are very fond of those you take to and would certainly prove to be a capable friend, even when things get quite tough.

In love relationships you are steadfast and reliable, and yet you never lose the ability to entertain. Yours is a dry sense of humour which shows itself to a multitude of different people and which doesn't run out, even on those occasions when life gets tough. It might take you a long time to find the love of your life, but when you do there is a greater possibility of retaining the relationship for a long period. You don't tend to inherit money, but you can easily make it for yourself, though you won't worry too much about the amount. On the whole you are a very self-sufficient and sensible individual.

Capricorn with Sagittarius Ascendant

THE MOON AND THE PART IT PLAYS IN YOUR LIFE

In astrology the Moon is probably the single most important heavenly body after the Sun. Its unique position, as partner to the Earth on its journey around the solar system, means that the Moon appears to pass through the signs of the zodiac extremely quickly. The zodiac position of the Moon at the time of your birth plays a great part in personal character and is especially significant in the build-up of your emotional nature.

Your Own Moon Sign

Discovering the position of the Moon at the time of your birth has always been notoriously difficult because tracking the complex zodiac positions of the Moon is not easy. This process has been reduced to three simple stages with our Lunar Tables. A breakdown of the Moon's zodiac positions can be found from page 35 onwards, so that once you know what your Moon Sign is, you can see what part this plays in the overall build-up of your personal character.

If you follow the instructions on the next page you will soon be able to work out exactly what zodiac sign the Moon occupied on the day that you were born and you can then go on to compare the reading for this position with those of your Sun sign and your Ascendant. It is partly the comparison between these three important positions that goes towards making you the unique individual you are.

How To Discover Your Moon Sign

This is a three-stage process. You may need a pen and a piece of paper but if you follow the instructions below the process should only take a minute or so.

STAGE 1 First of all you need to know the Moon Age at the time of your birth. If you look at Moon Table 1, on page 33, you will find all the years between 1921 and 2019 down the left side. Find the year of your birth and then trace across to the right to the month of your birth. Where the two intersect you will find a number. This is the date of the New Moon in the month that you were born. You now need to count forward the number of days between the New Moon and your own birthday. For example, if the New Moon in the month of your birth was shown as being the 6th and you were born on the 20th, your Moon Age Day would be 14. If the New Moon in the month of your birth came after your birthday, you need to count forward from the New Moon in the previous month, which, if you were born in January, means you must look at December in the previous year. You cannot count from December in the year of your birth, as that month is *after* your birth. Whatever the result, jot this number down so that you do not forget it.

STAGE 2 Take a look at Moon Table 2 on page 34. Down the left hand column look for the date of your birth. Now trace across to the month of your birth. Where the two meet you will find a letter. Copy this letter down alongside your Moon Age Day.

STAGE 3 Moon Table 3 on page 34 will supply you with the zodiac sign the Moon occupied on the day of your birth. Look for your Moon Age Day down the left hand column and then for the letter you found in Stage 2. Where the two converge you will find a zodiac sign and this is the sign occupied by the Moon on the day that you were born.

Your Zodiac Moon Sign Explained

You will find a profile of all zodiac Moon Signs on pages 35 to 38, showing in yet another way how astrology helps to make you into the individual that you are. In each daily entry of the Astral Diary you can find the zodiac position of the Moon for every day of the year. This also allows you to discover your lunar birthdays. Since the Moon passes through all the signs of the zodiac in about a month, you can expect something like twelve lunar birthdays each year. At these times you are likely to be emotionally steady and able to make the sort of decisions that have real, lasting value.

MOON TABLE 1

YEAR	NOV	DEC	JAN	YEAR	NOV	DEC	JAN	YEAR	NOV	DEC	JAN
1921	29	29	9	1954	25	25	5	1987	21	20	29
1922	19	18	27	1955	14	14	24	1988	9	9	19
1923	8	8	17	1956	2	2	13	1989	28	28	7
1924	26	26	6	1957	21	21 1/30		1990	17	17	26
1925	16	15	24	1958	11	10	19	1991	6	6	15
1926	5	5	14	1959	30	29	9	1992	24	24	4
1927	24	24	3	1960	19	18	27	1993	14	14	22
1928	12	12	21	1961	8	7	16	1994	3	2	11
1929	1 1/30		11	1962	27	26	6	1995	22	22	1
1930	20	19	29	1963	15	15	25	1996	11	10	20
1931	9	9	18	1964	4	4	14	1997	30	29	9
1932	27	27	7	1965	22	22	3	1998	19	18	28
1933	17	17	25	1966	12	12	21	1999	8	7	17
1934	7	6	15	1967	2	1/30	10	2000	27	25	6
1935	26	25	5	1968	21	20	29	2001	16	15	24
1936	14	13	24	1969	9	9	19	2002	4	4	13
1937	3	2	12	1970	29	28	7	2003	24	23	3
1938	22	21 1/31		1971	18	17	26	2004	11	11	21
1939	11	10	20	1972	6	6	15	2005	1	1	10
1940	29	28	9	1973	25	25	5	2006	20	20	29
1941	19	18	27	1974	14	14	24	2007	9	9	18
1942	8	8	16	1975	3	3	12	2008	28	27	8
1943	27	27	6	1976	21	21 1/31		2009	17	16	26
1944	15	15	25	1977	11	10	19	2010	6	6	15
1945	4	4	14	1978	30	29	9	2011	25	25	4
1946	23	23	3	1979	19	18	27	2012	13	12	23
1947	12	12	21	1980	8	7	16	2013	2	2	12
1948	1 1/30		11	1981	26	26	6	2014	22	22 1/31	
1949	20	19	29	1982	15	15	25	2015	11	20	19
1950	9	9	18	1983	4	4	14	2016	29	29	9
1951	29	28	7	1984	22	22	3	2017	18	18	27
1952	17	17	26	1985	12	12	21	2018	7	7	16
1953	6	6	15	1986	2	1/30	10	2019	26	26	5

TABLE 2   MOON TABLE 3

DAY	DEC	JAN	M/D	i	m	n	q	A	B	C
1	i	A	0	SA	SA	SA	CP	CP	AQ	AQ
2	i	A	1	SA	SA	CP	CP	AQ	AQ	AQ
3	m	A	2	CP	CP	CP	AQ	AQ	AQ	PI
4	m	A	3	CP	CP	AQ	AQ	AQ	PI	PI
5	n	A	4	CP	AQ	AQ	PI	PI	PI	AR
6	n	A	5	AQ	AQ	PI	PI	PI	AR	AR
7	n	A	6	AQ	AQ	PI	AR	AR	AR	AR
8	n	A	7	PI	PI	AR	AR	AR	AR	TA
9	n	A	8	PI	PI	AR	AR	AR	TA	TA
10	n	A	9	AR	AR	TA	TA	TA	TA	GE
11	n	B	10	AR	AR	TA	TA	TA	GE	GE
12	n	B	11	TA	TA	TA	GE	GE	GE	GE
13	n	B	12	TA	TA	GE	GE	GE	GE	CA
14	n	B	13	GE	GE	GE	GE	GE	CA	CA
15	n	B	14	GE	GE	CA	CA	CA	CA	LE
16	n	B	15	GE	GE	GE	CA	CA	LE	LE
17	n	B	16	GE	CA	CA	CA	LE	LE	LE
18	n	B	17	CA	CA	CA	LE	LE	LE	VI
19	n	B	18	CA	CA	LE	LE	LE	VI	VI
20	n	B	19	CA	LE	LE	LE	VI	VI	VI
21	n	C	20	LE	LE	LE	VI	VI	LI	LI
22	n	C	21	LE	LE	VI	VI	LI	LI	LI
23	q	C	22	VI	VI	VI	LI	LI	LI	SC
24	q	C	23	VI	VI	VI	LI	LI	SC	SC
25	q	C	24	VI	VI	LI	LI	SC	SC	SC
26	q	C	25	LI	LI	LI	SC	SC	SA	SA
27	q	C	26	LI	LI	SC	SC	SA	SA	SA
28	q	C	27	SC	SC	SC	SA	SA	SA	CP
29	q	C	28	SC	SC	SC	SA	SA	CP	CP
30	q	C	29	SC	SA	SA	SA	CP	CP	CP
31	q	C								

AR = Aries, TA = Taurus, GE = Gemini, CA = Cancer, LE = Leo, VI = Virgo,
LI = Libra, SC = Scorpio, SA = Sagittarius, CP = Capricorn, AQ = Aquarius, PI = Pisces

MOON SIGNS

Moon in Aries

You have a strong imagination, courage, determination and a desire to do things in your own way and forge your own path through life.

Originality is a key attribute; you are seldom stuck for ideas although your mind is changeable and you could take the time to focus on individual tasks. Often quick-tempered, you take orders from few people and live life at a fast pace. Avoid health problems by taking regular time out for rest and relaxation.

Emotionally, it is important that you talk to those you are closest to and work out your true feelings. Once you discover that people are there to help, there is less necessity for you to do everything yourself.

Moon in Taurus

The Moon in Taurus gives you a courteous and friendly manner, which means you are likely to have many friends.

The good things in life mean a lot to you, as Taurus is an Earth sign that delights in experiences which please the senses. Hence you are probably a lover of good food and drink, which may in turn mean you need to keep an eye on the bathroom scales, especially as looking good is also important to you.

Emotionally you are fairly stable and you stick by your own standards. Taureans do not respond well to change. Intuition also plays an important part in your life.

Moon in Gemini

You have a warm-hearted character, sympathetic and eager to help others. At times reserved, you can also be articulate and chatty: this is part of the paradox of Gemini, which always brings duplicity to the nature. You are interested in current affairs, have a good intellect, and are good company and likely to have many friends. Most of your friends have a high opinion of you and would be ready to defend you should the need arise. However, this is usually unnecessary, as you are quite capable of defending yourself in any verbal confrontation.

Travel is important to your inquisitive mind and you find intellectual stimulus in mixing with people from different cultures. You also gain much from reading, writing and the arts but you do need plenty of rest and relaxation in order to avoid fatigue.

Moon in Cancer

The Moon in Cancer at the time of birth is a fortunate position as Cancer is the Moon's natural home. This means that the qualities of compassion and understanding given by the Moon are especially enhanced in your nature, and you are friendly and sociable and cope well with emotional pressures. You cherish home and family life, and happily do the domestic tasks. Your surroundings are important to you and you hate squalor and filth. You are likely to have a love of music and poetry.

Your basic character, although at times changeable like the Moon itself, depends on symmetry. You aim to make your surroundings comfortable and harmonious, for yourself and those close to you.

Moon in Leo

The best qualities of the Moon and Leo come together to make you warm-hearted, fair, ambitious and self-confident. With good organisational abilities, you invariably rise to a position of responsibility in your chosen career. This is fortunate as you don't enjoy being an 'also-ran' and would rather be an important part of a small organisation than a menial in a large one.

You should be lucky in love, and happy, provided you put in the effort to make a comfortable home for yourself and those close to you. It is likely that you will have a love of pleasure, sport, music and literature. Life brings you many rewards, most of them as a direct result of your own efforts, although you may be luckier than average and ready to make the best of any situation.

Moon in Virgo

You are endowed with good mental abilities and a keen receptive memory, but you are never ostentatious or pretentious. Naturally quite reserved, you still have many friends, especially of the opposite sex. Marital relationships must be discussed carefully and worked at so that they remain harmonious, as personal attachments can be a problem if you do not give them your full attention.

Talented and persevering, you possess artistic qualities and are a good homemaker. Earning your honours through genuine merit, you work long and hard towards your objectives but show little pride in your achievements. Many short journeys will be undertaken in your life.

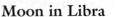

Moon in Libra

With the Moon in Libra you are naturally popular and make friends easily. People like you, probably more than you realise, you bring fun to a party and are a natural diplomat. For all its good points, Libra is not the most stable of astrological signs and, as a result, your emotions can be a little unstable too. Therefore, although the Moon in Libra is said to be good for love and marriage, your Sun sign and Rising sign will have an important effect on your emotional and loving qualities.

You must remember to relate to others in your decision-making. Co-operation is crucial because Libra represents the 'balance' of life that can only be achieved through harmonious relationships. Conformity is not easy for you because Libra, an Air sign, likes its independence.

Moon in Scorpio

Some people might call you pushy. In fact, all you really want to do is to live life to the full and protect yourself and your family from the pressures of life. Take care to avoid giving the impression of being sarcastic or impulsive and use your energies wisely and constructively.

You have great courage and you invariably achieve your goals by force of personality and sheer effort. You are fond of mystery and are good at predicting the outcome of situations and events. Travel experiences can be beneficial to you.

You may experience problems if you do not take time to examine your motives in a relationship, and also if you allow jealousy, always a feature of Scorpio, to cloud your judgement.

Moon in Sagittarius

The Moon in Sagittarius helps to make you a generous individual with humanitarian qualities and a kind heart. Restlessness may be intrinsic as your mind is seldom still. Perhaps because of this, you have a need for change that could lead you to several major moves during your adult life. You are not afraid to stand your ground when you know your judgement is right, you speak directly and have good intuition.

At work you are quick, efficient and versatile and so you make an ideal employee. You need work to be intellectually demanding and do not enjoy tedious routines.

In relationships, you anger quickly if faced with stupidity or deception, though you are just as quick to forgive and forget. Emotionally, there are times when your heart rules your head.

Moon in Capricorn

The Moon in Capricorn makes you popular and likely to come into the public eye in some way. The watery Moon is not entirely comfortable in the Earth sign of Capricorn and this may lead to some difficulties in the early years of life. An initial lack of creative ability and indecision must be overcome before the true qualities of patience and perseverance inherent in Capricorn can show through.

You have good administrative ability and are a capable worker, and if you are careful you can accumulate wealth. But you must be cautious and take professional advice in partnerships, as you are open to deception. You may be interested in social or welfare work, which suit your organisational skills and sympathy for others.

Moon in Aquarius

The Moon in Aquarius makes you an active and agreeable person with a friendly, easy-going nature. Sympathetic to the needs of others, you flourish in a laid-back atmosphere. You are broad-minded, fair and open to suggestion, although sometimes you have an unconventional quality which others can find hard to understand.

You are interested in the strange and curious, and in old articles and places. You enjoy trips to these places and gain much from them. Political, scientific and educational work interests you and you might choose a career in science or technology.

Money-wise, you make gains through innovation and concentration and Lunar Aquarians often tackle more than one job at a time. In love you are kind and honest.

Moon in Pisces

You have a kind, sympathetic nature, somewhat retiring at times, but you always take account of others' feelings and help when you can.

Personal relationships may be problematic, but as life goes on you can learn from your experiences and develop a better understanding of yourself and the world around you.

You have a fondness for travel, appreciate beauty and harmony and hate disorder and strife. You may be fond of literature and would make a good writer or speaker yourself. You have a creative imagination and may come across as an incurable romantic. You have strong intuition, maybe bordering on a mediumistic quality, which sets you apart from the mass. You may not be rich in cash terms, but your personal gifts are worth more than gold.

CAPRICORN IN LOVE

Discover how compatible in love you are with people from the same and other signs of the zodiac. Five stars equals a match made in heaven!

Capricorn meets Capricorn

One of the best combinations because Capricorn knows what it wants and likes its partner to be the same. This may not be the deepest or most passionate of relationships, but Capricorn is adaptable enough to accept that. Material success is likely for this couple as they share the ability to move slowly towards even distant horizons. There will be words of love and a generally happy family atmosphere, and although at times the relationship may look lukewarm, it will usually remain strong and secure. Star rating: *****

Capricorn meets Aquarius

Probably one of the least likely combinations as Capricorn and Aquarius are unlikely to choose each other in the first place, unless one side is quite untypical of their sign. Capricorn approaches things in a practical way and likes to get things done, while Aquarius works almost exclusively for the moment and relies heavily on intuition. Their attitudes to romance are also diametrically opposed: Aquarius' moods tend to swing from red hot to ice cold in a minute, which is alien to steady Capricorn. Star rating: **

Capricorn meets Pisces

There is some chance of a happy relationship here, but it will need work on both sides. Capricorn is a go-getter, but likes to plan long term. Pisces is naturally more immediate, but has enough intuition to understand the Goat's thinking. Both have patience, but it will usually be Pisces who chooses to play second fiddle. The quiet nature of both signs might be a problem, as someone will have to lead, especially in social situations. Both signs should recognise this fact and accommodate it. Star rating: ***

Capricorn meets Aries

Capricorn works conscientiously to achieve its objectives and so can be the perfect companion for Aries. The Ram knows how to achieve but not how to consolidate, so the two signs have a great deal to offer one another practically. There may not be fireworks and it's sometimes doubtful how well they know each other, but it may not matter. Aries is outwardly hot but inwardly cool, whilst Capricorn can appear low-key but be a furnace underneath. Such a pairing can gradually find contentment, though both parties may wonder how this is so. Star rating: ****

Capricorn meets Taurus

If not quite a match made in heaven, this comes close. Both signs are Earthy in nature and that is a promising start. Capricorn is very practical and can make a Taurean's dreams come true. Both are tidy, like to know what is going to happen in a day-to-day sense, and are steady and committed. Taurus loves refinement, which Capricorn accepts and even helps to create. A good prognosis for material success rounds off a relationship that could easily stay the course. The only thing missing is a genuine sense of humour. Star rating: *****

Capricorn meets Gemini

Gemini has a natural fondness for Capricorn, which at first may be mutual. However, Capricorn is very organised, practical and persevering, and always achieves its goals in the end. Gemini starts out like this, but then starts to use a more instinctive and evolutionary approach, which may interfere with mutual objectives. To compensate, Gemini helps Capricorn avoid taking itself too seriously, while Capricorn brings a degree of stability into Gemini's world. When this pairing does work, though, it will be spectacular! Star rating: ***

Capricorn meets Cancer

Just about the only thing this pair have in common is the fact that both signs begin 'Ca'! Some signs of the zodiac are instigators and some are reactors, and both the Crab and the Goat are reactors. Consequently, they both need incentives from their partners but won't find it in each other and, with neither side taking the initiative, there's a spark missing. Cancer and Capricorn do think alike in some ways and so, if they can find their common purpose, they can be as happy as anyone. It's just rather unlikely. Star rating: **

Capricorn meets Leo

Despite promising appearances, this match often fails to take. Capricorn focuses on long-term objectives and, like Leo, is very practical. Both signs are capable of attaining success after a struggle, which, while requiring effort, gives them a mutual goal. But when life is easier, the cracks begin to show. Capricorn can be too serious for Leo, and the couple share few ideals. Leo loves luxury, Capricorn seeks austerity. Leo is warm but Capricorn seems cold and wintry in comparison. Both have many good points, but they don't seem to fire each other off properly. Star rating: **

Capricorn meets Virgo

One of the best possible combinations, because Virgo and Capricorn have an instinctive understanding. Both signs know the value of dedicated hard work and apply it equally in a relationship and other areas of life. Two of the most practical signs, nothing is beyond their ken, even if to outsiders they appear rather sterile or lacking in 'oomph'. What matters most is that the individuals are happy and with so much in common, the likelihood of mutual material success, and a shared devotion to home and family, there isn't much doubt of that. Star rating: *****

Capricorn meets Libra

Libra and Capricorn rub each other up the wrong way because their attitudes to life are so different, and although both are capable of doing something about this, in reality they probably won't. Capricorn is steady, determined and solid, while Libra is bright but sometimes superficial and not entirely reliable. They usually lack the instant spark needed to get them together in the first place, so when it does happen it is often because one of the partners is not very typical of their sign. Star rating: **

Capricorn meets Scorpio

Lack of communication is the governing factor here. Neither of this pair are renowned communicators and both need a partner to draw out their full verbal potential. Consequently, Scorpio may find Capricorn cold and unapproachable while Capricorn could find Scorpio dark and brooding. Both are naturally tidy and would keep a pristine house but great effort and a mutual goal is needed on both sides to overcome the missing spark. A good match on the financial side, but probably not an earth-shattering personal encounter. Star rating: **

Capricorn meets Sagittarius

Any real problem here will stem from a lack of understanding. Capricorn is very practical and needs to be constantly on the go – though in a fairly low-key sort of way. Sagittarius is busy too, though always in a panic and invariably behind its deadlines, which will annoy organised Capricorn. Sagittarius doesn't really have the depth of nature that best suits an Earth sign like Capricorn and its flirty nature could upset the sensitive Goat, but their lighter attitude could be cheering, too. Star rating: ***

VENUS:
THE PLANET OF LOVE

If you look up at the sky around sunset or sunrise you will often see Venus in close attendance to the Sun. It is arguably one of the most beautiful sights of all and there is little wonder that historically it became associated with the goddess of love. But although Venus is important in your attitude to love and in the way others see you romantically, this is only one of its spheres of influence.

Venus plays a part in the cultured side of your life and has much to do with your appreciation of art, literature, music and general creativity. Even the way you look is responsive to the part of the zodiac that Venus occupied at the start of your life, though this is also down to your Sun sign and Ascending sign. If, at the time you were born, Venus occupied one of the more gregarious zodiac signs, you will be open in love, as well as more attracted to entertainment, social gatherings and good company. If on the other hand Venus occupied a quiet zodiac sign at the time of your birth, you would tend to be more retiring and less willing to shine in public situations.

Venus can have a great bearing on your outward appearance and since we all have to mix with others, knowledge of Venus' position at your birth can help you learn to make the best of what it has to offer you.

One of the great complications in the past has always been trying to establish exactly what zodiac position Venus enjoyed when you were born because the planet is notoriously difficult to track. Here we have created an exclusive table for your Sun sign, shown on the next page.

To calculate your Venus sign, first look up the year of your birth in the table. As Capricorn naturally spans two calendar years every time it comes around, double-check that you are looking at the right line. The table is organised so that December is always the first month, so, for instance, if you were born in December 1940 or January 1941 you would look at the row for 1940–1, because the year on the calendar has changed while the zodiac is still in the sign of Capricorn. If you were born in January 1942 you would look at the row for 1941–2. Once you have the right row, you will see a sign of the zodiac next to the date. This was the sign that Venus occupied in that year. If Venus occupied more than one sign during the period, this is indicated by the date on which the sign changed and the name of the new sign. For instance, if you are looking at the years 1940–1, Venus was in Sagittarius until the 15th January, after which time it was in Capricorn. If you were born before 15th January your Venus sign is Sagittarius, if you were born on or after 15th January, your Venus sign is Capricorn. Once you have established the position of Venus at the time of your birth, you can then look in the pages which follow to see how this has a bearing on your life.

1921–2 SAGITTARIUS/30.12 CAPRICORN
1922–3 SCORPIO/6.1 SAGITTARIUS
1923–4 CAPRICORN/
     26.12 AQUARIUS/19.1 PISCES
1924–5 SAGITTARIUS/15.1 CAPRICORN
1925–6 AQUARIUS
1926–7 CAPRICORN/9.1 AQUARIUS
1927–8 SCORPIO/4.1 SAGITTARIUS
1928–9 AQUARIUS/6.1 PISCES
1929–30 SAGITTARIUS/29.12
     CAPRICORN
1930–1 SCORPIO/3.1 SAGITTARIUS
1931–2 CAPRICORN/
     26.12 AQUARIUS/19.1 PISCES
1932–3 SAGITTARIUS/15.1 PISCES
1933–4 AQUARIUS
1934–5 CAPRICORN/9.1 AQUARIUS
1935–6 SCORPIO/4.1 SAGITTARIUS
1936–7 AQUARIUS/6.1 PISCES
1937–8 SAGITTARIUS/29.12 CAPRICORN
1938–9 SCORPIO/3.1 SAGITTARIUS
1939–40 CAPRICORN/
     25.12 AQUARIUS/18.1 PISCES
1940–1 SAGITTARIUS/15.1 CAPRICORN
1941–2 AQUARIUS
1942–3 CAPRICORN/8.1 AQUARIUS
1943–4 SCORPIO/3.1 SAGITTARIUS
1944–5 AQUARIUS/5.1 PISCES
1945–6 SAGITTARIUS/28.12 CAPRICORN
1946–7 SCORPIO/3.1 SAGITTARIUS
1947–8 CAPRICORN/
     25.12 AQUARIUS/18.1 PISCES
1948–9 SAGITTARIUS/14.1 CAPRICORN
1949–50 AQUARIUS
1950–1 CAPRICORN/8.1 AQUARIUS
1951–2 SCORPIO/3.1 SAGITTARIUS
1952–3 AQUARIUS/5.1 PISCES
1953–4 SAGITTARIUS/28.12 CAPRICORN
1954–5 SCORPIO/4.1 SAGITTARIUS
1955–6 CAPRICORN/
     24.12 AQUARIUS/17.1 PISCES
1956–7 SAGITTARIUS/14.1 CAPRICORN
1957–8 AQUARIUS
1958–9 CAPRICORN/7.1 AQUARIUS
1959–60 SCORPIO/2.1 SAGITTARIUS
1960–1 AQUARIUS/5.1 PISCES
1961–2 SAGITTARIUS/28.12 CAPRICORN
1962–3 SCORPIO/4.1 SAGITTARIUS
1963–4 CAPRICORN/
     24.12 AQUARIUS/17.1 PISCES
1964–5 SAGITTARIUS/13.1 CAPRICORN
1965–6 AQUARIUS
1966–7 CAPRICORN/7.1 AQUARIUS
1967–8 SCORPIO/2.1 SAGITTARIUS
1968–9 AQUARIUS/5.1 PISCES
1969–70 SAGITTARIUS/
     27.12 CAPRICORN
1970–1 SCORPIO/5.1 SAGITTARIUS

1971–2 CAPRICORN/
     23.12 AQUARIUS/16.1 PISCES
1972–3 SAGITTARIUS/12.1 CAPRICORN
1973–4 AQUARIUS
1974–5 CAPRICORN/6.1 AQUARIUS
1975–6 SCORPIO/1.1 SAGITTARIUS
1976–7 AQUARIUS/4.1 PISCES
1977–8 SAGITTARIUS/27.12 CAPRICORN
1978–9 SCORPIO/5.1 SAGITTARIUS
1979–80 CAPRICORN/
     23.12 AQUARIUS/16.1 PISCES
1980–1 SAGITTARIUS/12.1 CAPRICORN
1981–2 AQUARIUS
1982–3 CAPRICORN/6.1 AQUARIUS
1983–4 SCORPIO/1.1 SAGITTARIUS
1984–5 AQUARIUS/4.1 PISCES
1985–6 SAGITTARIUS/27.12 CAPRICORN
1986–7 SCORPIO/6.1 SAGITTARIUS
1987–8 AQUARIUS/15.1 PISCES
1988–9 SAGITTARIUS/11.1 CAPRICORN
1989–90 AQUARIUS/17.1 CAPRICORN
1990–1 CAPRICORN/5.1 AQUARIUS
1991–2 SCORPIO/1.1 SAGITTARIUS
1992–3 AQUARIUS/4.1 PISCES
1993–4 SAGITTARIUS/26.12 CAPRICORN
1994–5 SCORPIO/7.1 SAGITTARIUS
1995–6 AQUARIUS/15.1 PISCES
1996–7 SAGITTARIUS/11.1 CAPRICORN
1997–8 AQUARIUS/14.1 CAPRICORN
1998–9 CAPRICORN/5.1 AQUARIUS
1999–2000 SCORPIO/1.1 SAGITTARIUS
2000–01 SAGITTARIUS/
     26.12 CAPRICORN
2001–02 CAPRICORN/4.1 AQUARIUS
2002–03 SAGITTARIUS/
     26.12 CAPRICORN
2003–04 SCORPIO/7.1 SAGITTARIUS
2004–05 SAGITTARIUS/
     30.12 CAPRICORN
2005–06 AQUARIUS / 2.1 CAPRICORN
2006–07 AQUARIUS/14.1 CAPRICORN
2007–08 CAPRICORN / 5.1 AQUARIUS
2008–09 SCORPIO / 1.1 SAGITTARIUS
2009–10 SAGITTARIUS /
     26.12 CAPRICORN
2010–11 SAGITTARIUS/
     26.12 CAPRICORN
2011–12 CAPRICORN / 4.12 AQUARIUS
2012–13 AQUARIUS/14.1 CAPRICORN
2013–14 CAPRICORN / 5.1 AQUARIUS
2014–15 AQUARIUS/14.1 CAPRICORN
2015–16 CAPRICORN / 5.1 AQUARIUS
2016–17 AQUARIUS / 1.1 SAGITTARIUS
2017 SAGITTARIUS / 26.12 CAPRICORN
2018 SAGITTARIUS / 26.12 CAPRICORN
2019–2020 CAPRICORN/ 4.12 AQUARIUS

VENUS THROUGH THE ZODIAC SIGNS

Venus in Aries

Amongst other things, the position of Venus in Aries indicates a fondness for travel, music and all creative pursuits. Your nature tends to be affectionate and you would try not to create confusion or difficulty for others if it could be avoided. Many people with this planetary position have a great love of the theatre, and mental stimulation is of the greatest importance. Early romantic attachments are common with Venus in Aries, so it is very important to establish a genuine sense of romantic continuity. Early marriage is not recommended, especially if it is based on sympathy. You may give your heart a little too readily on occasions.

Venus in Taurus

You are capable of very deep feelings and your emotions tend to last for a very long time. This makes you a trusting partner and lover, whose constancy is second to none. In life you are precise and careful and always try to do things the right way. Although this means an ordered life, which you are comfortable with, it can also lead you to be rather too fussy for your own good. Despite your pleasant nature, you are very fixed in your opinions and quite able to speak your mind. Others are attracted to you and historical astrologers always quoted this position of Venus as being very fortunate in terms of marriage. However, if you find yourself involved in a failed relationship, it could take you a long time to trust again.

Venus in Gemini

As with all associations related to Gemini, you tend to be quite versatile, anxious for change and intelligent in your dealings with the world at large. You may gain money from more than one source but you are equally good at spending it. There is an inference here that you are a good communicator, via either the written or the spoken word, and you love to be in the company of interesting people. Always on the look-out for culture, you may also be very fond of music, and love to indulge the curious and cultured side of your nature. In romance you tend to have more than one relationship and could find yourself associated with someone who has previously been a friend or even a distant relative.

Venus in Cancer

You often stay close to home because you are very fond of family and enjoy many of your most treasured moments when you are with those you love. Being naturally sympathetic, you will always do anything you can to support those around you, even people you hardly know at all. This charitable side of your nature is your most noticeable trait and is one of the reasons why others are naturally so fond of you. Being receptive and in some cases even psychic, you can see through to the soul of most of those with whom you come into contact. You may not commence too many romantic attachments but when you do give your heart, it tends to be unconditionally.

Venus in Leo

It must become quickly obvious to almost anyone you meet that you are kind, sympathetic and yet determined enough to stand up for anyone or anything that is truly important to you. Bright and sunny, you warm the world with your natural enthusiasm and would rarely do anything to hurt those around you, or at least not intentionally. In romance you are ardent and sincere, though some may find your style just a little overpowering. Gains come through your contacts with other people and this could be especially true with regard to romance, for love and money often come hand in hand for those who were born with Venus in Leo. People claim to understand you, though you are more complex than you seem.

Venus in Virgo

Your nature could well be fairly quiet no matter what your Sun sign might be, though this fact often manifests itself as an inner peace and would not prevent you from being basically sociable. Some delays and even the odd disappointment in love cannot be ruled out with this planetary position, though it's a fact that you will usually find the happiness you look for in the end. Catapulting yourself into romantic entanglements that you know to be rather ill-advised is not sensible, and it would be better to wait before you committed yourself exclusively to any one person. It is the essence of your nature to serve the world at large and through doing so it is possible that you will attract money at some stage in your life.

Venus in Libra

Venus is very comfortable in Libra and bestows upon those people who have this planetary position a particular sort of kindness that is easy to recognise. This is a very good position for all sorts of friendships and also for romantic attachments that usually bring much joy into your life. Few individuals with Venus in Libra would avoid marriage and since you are capable of great depths of love, it is likely that you will find a contented personal life. You like to mix with people of integrity and intelligence but don't take kindly to scruffy surroundings or work that means getting your hands too dirty. Careful speculation, good business dealings and money through marriage all seem fairly likely.

Venus in Scorpio

You are quite open and tend to spend money quite freely, even on those occasions when you don't have very much. Although your intentions are always good, there are times when you get yourself in to the odd scrape and this can be particularly true when it comes to romance, which you may come to late or from a rather unexpected direction. Certainly you have the power to be happy and to make others contented on the way, but you find the odd stumbling block on your journey through life and it could seem that you have to work harder than those around you. As a result of this, you gain a much deeper understanding of the true value of personal happiness than many people ever do, and are likely to achieve true contentment in the end.

Venus in Sagittarius

You are lighthearted, cheerful and always able to see the funny side of any situation. These facts enhance your popularity, which is especially high with members of the opposite sex. You should never have to look too far to find romantic interest in your life, though it is just possible that you might be too willing to commit yourself before you are certain that the person in question is right for you. Part of the problem here extends to other areas of life too. The fact is that you like variety in everything and so can tire of situations that fail to offer it. All the same, if you choose wisely and learn to understand your restless side, then great happiness can be yours.

Venus in Capricorn

The most notable trait that comes from Venus in this position is that it makes you trustworthy and able to take on all sorts of responsibilities in life. People are instinctively fond of you and love you all the more because you are always ready to help those who are in any form of need. Social and business popularity can be yours and there is a magnetic quality to your nature that is particularly attractive in a romantic sense. Anyone who wants a partner for a lover, a spouse and a good friend too would almost certainly look in your direction. Constancy is the hallmark of your nature and unfaithfulness would go right against the grain. You might sometimes be a little too trusting.

Venus in Aquarius

This location of Venus offers a fondness for travel and a desire to try out something new at every possible opportunity. You are extremely easy to get along with and tend to have many friends from varied backgrounds, classes and inclinations. You like to live a distinct sort of life and gain a great deal from moving about, both in a career sense and with regard to your home. It is not out of the question that you could form a romantic attachment to someone who comes from far away or be attracted to a person of a distinctly artistic and original nature. What you cannot stand is jealousy, for you have friends of both sexes and would want to keep things that way.

Venus in Pisces

The first thing people tend to notice about you is your wonderful, warm smile. Being very charitable by nature you will do anything to help others, even if you don't know them well. Much of your life may be spent sorting out situations for other people, but it is very important to feel that you are living for yourself too. In the main, you remain cheerful, and tend to be quite attractive to members of the opposite sex. Where romantic attachments are concerned, you could be drawn to people who are significantly older or younger than yourself or to someone with a unique career or point of view. It might be best for you to avoid marrying whilst you are still very young.

CAPRICORN:
2018 DIARY PAGES

October 2018

1 MONDAY
Moon Age Day 22   Moon Sign Gemini

You should find it easier to get your own way this week. If there are issues that you feel need resolving, especially in the personal sphere, now is the time to tackle them head on. In a financial sense, some of the finer things in life that you have been hoping might come your way are not likely to be all that far away.

2 TUESDAY
Moon Age Day 23   Moon Sign Cancer

There could be a slightly sluggish start to today, brought about in the main by the lunar low. However, the demands you make of life are not all that great and if you keep a fairly low profile the lunar low may pass you by quietly. Seek new forms of entertainment and keep your mind occupied if you can.

3 WEDNESDAY
Moon Age Day 24   Moon Sign Cancer

Curb your ambitions as much as possible and leave some of the major decisions that are waiting in the wings for just a little longer. Dig out information from the past when it seems obvious that your former actions can have a bearing on the present but don't let yourself become too nostalgic because some sorrow could be the result.

4 THURSDAY
Moon Age Day 25   Moon Sign Leo

Today should be good in terms of your resources because you are likely to get on top of your spending and could coming up with some ingenious plans to hang on to money in the medium and long-term. You have the ability to look far ahead of yourself at this time and will be almost prophetic in your thoughts and actions.

5 FRIDAY
Moon Age Day 26   Moon Sign Leo

It appears that you will now be more anxious than ever to learn and to put what you have learned to good use in very practical ways. You remain extremely receptive to other people's ideas and will be able to move comfortably towards major objectives. You won't try to do everything all at once because you have patience par excellence.

6 SATURDAY
Moon Age Day 27   Moon Sign Virgo

Standing up for what you believe is right should not be too difficult under present trends and you can be quite courageous when the will takes you. This is more likely to be the case when you are defending those you love and since this is also a great time for romance it is likely to be the sphere of personal attachments that you prosper.

7 SUNDAY
Moon Age Day 28   Moon Sign Virgo

A positive belief in your own worth is vitally important if you want to wring as much as you can out of practical and business matters at this time. If you stand around, jumping from foot to foot, rivals may slip in and steal the prize. You need to be decisive but also to appear as cool as possible. It's a tall order but achievable.

8 MONDAY
Moon Age Day 29   Moon Sign Virgo

There is a continued emphasis on work and productivity and this must surely mean that things are happening around you. You have a big attitude to life at the moment and you may even be quite dramatic in the way you do things. People love to see the passionate side of your nature on display.

9 TUESDAY
Moon Age Day 0   Moon Sign Libra

Although rules and regulations might tend to get on your nerves you will realise, as you always do, that these are necessary to your happiness. It is likely that you will be quite original in your thinking, especially at work, and you show your very practical side on most occasions. Save time later in the day for important words of love.

10 WEDNESDAY   *Moon Age Day 1   Moon Sign Libra*

Patience is the keyword for Capricorn now. Everything you want can come your way eventually but much of it will be nothing more than potential under present trends. If you rush your fences now you might prevent an eventual success, whereas watching and waiting until the right moment will ensure you get what you are seeking.

11 THURSDAY   *Moon Age Day 2   Moon Sign Scorpio*

Dream up new and important projects for the future and lay the foundations of later actions one by one. Today can offer significant social diversion and you may have a great desire to be outdoors. From a physical point of view you could become involved in sporting activities, especially team sports.

12 FRIDAY   *Moon Age Day 3   Moon Sign Scorpio*

Though progress is now likely to be swift there is so much happening at the same time you may need a little assistance in order to make the best of it all. That means relying on other people, something you are occasionally loath to do. This stems from a feeling that if you want something doing right you must do it yourself – but this isn't the case.

13 SATURDAY   *Moon Age Day 4   Moon Sign Sagittarius*

You would certainly rather speak than listen today, which is why you have so much to say in almost any situation. Part of this is a nervous response on your part and it is also the case that you want to feel you are in command of everything. If there are things you don't understand today you could become quite frustrated.

14 SUNDAY   *Moon Age Day 5   Moon Sign Sagittarius*

You can protect your sense of your own identity in an original way today and may inspire others through your ability to be unique and to constantly turn in directions they don't expect. This should assure you of attention but will also lead to significant successes in your life. Little things turn your way under present trends and make for an interesting time.

15 MONDAY
Moon Age Day 6   Moon Sign Capricorn

Opportunities for expansion come along as the Moon races into your own sign of Capricorn. This is the time of the month to commit yourself to new projects and to show just how confident you are capable of being. The more you extend yourself the greater is the degree of confidence and help that is going to come from other people.

16 TUESDAY
Moon Age Day 7   Moon Sign Capricorn

This is one of the best days of the month for making important decisions and you won't want to be left behind when there is excitement on offer. Not only will you be very confident but it is likely that you will feel on top from in a physical sense too. Good fortune can play an important part in the way things pan out, especially at work.

17 WEDNESDAY
Moon Age Day 8   Moon Sign Capricorn

This ought to be a very favourable time indeed for getting on with those around you in a general sense. If not all the conversations you are having seem to possess the depth you would wish, who cares? There is nothing wrong with a little superficiality, just as long as you get what you need in the end. Stay cheerful and optimistic today.

18 THURSDAY
Moon Age Day 9   Moon Sign Aquarius

You may feel today that the pressure is somehow on in terms of relationships. This could show itself in any one of a number of different ways. Perhaps family members are more demanding, or your partner is worrying about specific issues. Whatever turns up, deal with it steadily and don't panic about anything.

19 FRIDAY
Moon Age Day 10   Moon Sign Aquarius

Your ability to attract just the right sort of people at this time is noteworthy. Keep yourself active, happy and geared towards situations that are reasonable. Friends should be of greater assistance now and they offer you the chance to follow a course of action that has seemed out of the question recently.

20 SATURDAY
Moon Age Day 11   Moon Sign Pisces

You might have to give in to other people today more than you would wish but to be willing to do this now means greater progress later. Personal attachments should be looking especially good and you will have the time today to follow up on a couple of issues that have been put on the back burner since before last weekend.

21 SUNDAY
Moon Age Day 12   Moon Sign Pisces

Discussions with others ought to prove fairly interesting today. If you do not work on a Sunday there is scope for social trends to win out. Maybe you are planning a family trip or a party? Whatever you turn your mind to now should be successful later. Your cheerfulness impresses everyone.

22 MONDAY
Moon Age Day 13   Moon Sign Pisces

You may now be entering a slightly up and down sort of period but it is one that offers all sorts of new incentives and plenty of diversity. If there are issues that need dealing with today you can be sure that you will sort these out quite quickly, especially if you are willing to fall back on the experience of relatives.

23 TUESDAY
Moon Age Day 14   Moon Sign Aries

Beware of getting hold of the wrong end of the stick when it comes to a personal matter. Although you think you are listening to others, you are probably not hearing exactly what they are trying to tell you. There are some deceptions around today, mostly coming from colleagues or people you don't know well.

24 WEDNESDAY
Moon Age Day 15   Moon Sign Aries

All you require today in order to make life go with a swing is a little extra incentive and some positive thinking. If things are not sorted out the way you would wish them to be, this is the time to put in that extra effort to help yourself. There are offers of support from colleagues and friends but you might not want to accept it.

25 THURSDAY   *Moon Age Day 16   Moon Sign Taurus*

Iron out problems with colleagues and make sure you do so before you move forward into a potential minefield of issues. Today is probably not the best time for concerted action because you tend to be in a very thoughtful frame of mind. Wait until tomorrow before you really begin to apply the pressure to any situation.

26 FRIDAY   *Moon Age Day 17   Moon Sign Taurus*

You are motivated by all sorts of new ideas and incentives at the end of this working week and there isn't any doubt that you have a great deal to contribute in a general sense. Not everyone understands what you are talking about today so in amongst the successes it would be worth explaining yourself just a little more carefully.

27 SATURDAY   *Moon Age Day 18   Moon Sign Gemini*

The daily routine will offer you a sense of stability and peace. Feeling at ease with yourself, you should be equally comfortable with everyone else around you. You enjoy their company and can make the most of the strong social trends that are surrounding you on all sides. Personal attachments should also look quite secure.

28 SUNDAY   *Moon Age Day 19   Moon Sign Gemini*

Any negotiations should proceed quickly and easily, mainly because you are so accommodating and also willing to stretch your own ideas to encompass those of other people. Hybrid solutions work extremely well and Capricorn is so co-operative at this time you could be forming alliances with unexpected people.

29 MONDAY   *Moon Age Day 20   Moon Sign Cancer*

You may feel a little unsure today and probably not on top form at the start of another week. The lunar low could hold you back a little and it could seem as though the things you want the most are still a long way off. By the middle of the week everything will look different so just exercise a little patience now.

30 TUESDAY   *Moon Age Day 21   Moon Sign Cancer*

Although you will want to make some necessary changes today, the time is probably not quite right yet. Look at situations today and do all the planning you want but wait for a while before you put your plans into action. This is because you will soon find new ways to cope with issues that are still puzzling you at the moment.

31 WEDNESDAY   *Moon Age Day 22   Moon Sign Cancer*

Good intuition should enable you to see ahead of yourself and will prevent you from making some of the mistakes that could come along otherwise. Turn up the heat of your love and let your special one know how you are feeling and continue to show as much of a co-operative spirit as you can. This is a mixed day but a good one.

November
2018

1 THURSDAY
Moon Age Day 23   Moon Sign Leo

You are possessed of considerable mental talents at the best of times but this really shows now. This is a time to stretch yourself and to explore new avenues. Your objectives may be self-evident but what matters around now is the newer and better ways you think up to get where you want to be.

2 FRIDAY
Moon Age Day 24   Moon Sign Leo

You have a need for communication of all kinds and a desire to get on with life to its fullest. There are several planets now contributing to the push you are about to make and with everything going your way, be willing to urge yourself forward. This might not always be easy but it certainly seems to be necessary.

3 SATURDAY
Moon Age Day 25   Moon Sign Virgo

All areas of communication should still be going well and this weekend could be especially important when it comes to getting what you want from love. Your popularity is hardly in doubt and Capricorns who are looking for a new romance should concentrate their efforts on social contacts and invitations this weekend.

4 SUNDAY
Moon Age Day 26   Moon Sign Virgo

A communicative trend makes you cheerful and approachable. Not everyone you get on well with today will be a person you have taken to in the past. You might have to re-write the book regarding your likes and dislikes of certain individuals and you could even discover a former adversary who is happy to join forces with you.

5 MONDAY   *Moon Age Day 27   Moon Sign Libra*

Someone at home could be making life more vibrant for you around now. There is excitement in the air and it is coming from a number of different directions. Stay loyal to the people who have been kind to you in the past and include them in your present schemes. Don't get too carried away with your own importance in a social sense.

6 TUESDAY   *Moon Age Day 28   Moon Sign Libra*

What loved ones have to offer today ought to be doubly reassuring but keep certain plans under wraps until you are more certain of your own potential success. If you play your hand too soon you could end up sharing your gains with too many people. Stick to those individuals who have always been loyal to you in the past.

7 WEDNESDAY   *Moon Age Day 0   Moon Sign Scorpio*

Expect a harmonious time, especially in the way you are getting on with loved ones, friends and colleagues alike. You have what it takes to heal breaches, even if they are ones you did nothing to create in the first place. Capricorn is now not likely to apportion blame to anyone or hold a grudge.

8 THURSDAY   *Moon Age Day 1   Moon Sign Scorpio*

You should now discover that attracting the money you need is somewhat easier, partly because others have so much confidence in what you have to say. Your own private nest egg should be growing and if you check all the accounts carefully it is quite possible you will discover you are better off then you thought.

9 FRIDAY   *Moon Age Day 2   Moon Sign Sagittarius*

You should not allow anything to interfere with the normal flow of business. This is an excellent time to emphasise how practical you are capable of being and it looks as though a wealth of people will be offering their own resources to support you. Not everyone is presently on your side but the people who really matter should be.

10 SATURDAY   *Moon Age Day 3   Moon Sign Sagittarius*

You now have a much better insight into your own thinking and it could be that you begin to realise important things about yourself that haven't occurred to you before. Domestic relationships should be especially rewarding but you also need to be out there in the wider world so it is vital that you split your time successfully today.

11 SUNDAY   *Moon Age Day 4   Moon Sign Sagittarius*

Work and money matters are positively highlighted right now and it looks as though you will find that getting what you want from life is significantly easier at this stage of November than sometimes seems to be the case. In reality you are moving small mountains without realising that they even exist!

12 MONDAY   *Moon Age Day 5   Moon Sign Capricorn*

This may prove to be one of your busiest periods as far as work is concerned. With plenty to think about and everything to play for you are likely to be right on form and keen to show your mettle. You won't rely on good luck because you are working so hard but don't be surprised if things turn your way more or less of their own accord.

13 TUESDAY   *Moon Age Day 6   Moon Sign Capricorn*

Casual conversations and communications of all sorts can be turned in a moment to your advantage and you show all day long just how ingenious you are. There are new starts in the offing, not to mention situations that test you to the full. All in all, you should positively enjoy what life throws at you.

14 WEDNESDAY   *Moon Age Day 7   Moon Sign Aquarius*

At home it looks as though emotional extremes might be somewhat difficult to avoid. A minor crisis could at least release pent-up emotions and you are almost certain to speak your mind at the moment, no matter what the implications might be. Get together with like-minded friends to ring the changes and reduce the intensity.

15 THURSDAY   *Moon Age Day 8   Moon Sign Aquarius*

You may be bored by your own domestic routines so look for inventive ways to get the most from all that is happening around you now. It is possible that you are failing to pick up on a number of opportunities and you need to look carefully at all the new possibilities that are starting to gather around you.

16 FRIDAY   *Moon Age Day 9   Moon Sign Aquarius*

The pull of the past is likely to be very strong today and you will be fairly nostalgic about certain events. This isn't an entirely bad thing because there are possible lessons to be learned for the future. In relationships you are loyal and not at all demanding, which seems to indicate a good period romantically.

17 SATURDAY   ☿   *Moon Age Day 10   Moon Sign Pisces*

You can make this a time of positive change, even if you have to take care not to try and move forward in too many areas at the same time. Friends have good ideas, some of which you will want to help them explore and it looks as though some quite fascinating news could come in from the direction of someone you don't know yet.

18 SUNDAY   ☿   *Moon Age Day 11   Moon Sign Pisces*

Make plans today and set out to learn new skills. Don't allow yourself to be held back by irrelevant details and look at the overall picture for once. Sunday should be good for your social life, and you have a good ability at this time to mix business with pleasure – to your definite profit.

19 MONDAY   ☿   *Moon Age Day 12   Moon Sign Aries*

Though you might have to overcome a slight sense of inertia at the beginning of this week you can gain ground in terms of domestic issues. If you feel you want to be more comfortable ahead of the winter, this might be a good time to make alterations at home. Some DIY should appeal to you now.

20 TUESDAY   ☿   *Moon Age Day 13   Moon Sign Aries*

The main area of pleasure and fulfilment remains with your home and family. Of course you cannot be there all the time but even when you are not, that is the direction in which your thoughts tend to run. Personal attachments seem to offer a greater sense of security than ever – which is something Capricorn always needs.

21 WEDNESDAY ☿   *Moon Age Day 14   Moon Sign Taurus*

There could be fruitful encounters with a range of different people today, some of whom have an important message to pass to you. Gradually, you should notice that things are speeding up. There are gains to be made in terms of your money-making potential and your thought processes are likely to be keener than ever.

22 THURSDAY   ☿   *Moon Age Day 15   Moon Sign Taurus*

Financial, legal and career matters should all be going quite well. If the time has come to sign documents of any sort or to take on a new commitment, you are in the best frame of mind to deal with such issues right now. Friends should be supportive and on occasions probably rather too helpful for your liking.

23 FRIDAY   ☿   *Moon Age Day 16   Moon Sign Taurus*

Positive thinking rules today and that has to be good for Capricorn, which sometimes lacks the ultimate commitment to move ahead in a confident way. Even when you are not sure of something, nobody around you would guess at the moment. You can bluff your way through anything and gain more and more confidence as you move forward.

24 SATURDAY   ☿   *Moon Age Day 17   Moon Sign Gemini*

Relationships with family members could improve – even if you aren't especially aware that anything has been wrong with them. In one or two cases there might have been a certain distance developing in what was once a water-tight attachment and you should soon see that everything is back to normal. Look after cash today.

25 SUNDAY ☿ *Moon Age Day 18   Moon Sign Gemini*

Along with a greater sense of self-determination, your energy levels pick up today. You are likely to be the main attraction in social groups and will be happy to occupy that position. Any doubts or uncertainties are left behind and you move forward in the knowledge that you really do know what you are doing.

26 MONDAY ☿ *Moon Age Day 19   Moon Sign Cancer*

You may struggle to achieve your ends for a couple of days but that doesn't mean you should avoid putting in the effort or give up altogether. Even moderate progress is better than no movement at all. Later in the day, set plenty of time aside to rest while the lunar low is around.

27 TUESDAY ☿ *Moon Age Day 20   Moon Sign Cancer*

Now is not the time to allow your confidence to get out of control. There are certain ideas that are presently sloshing about in your mind and this quiet spell gives you the chance to review them one by one. You may be slightly socially reluctant and will probably find your own fireside to be the most appealing place outside of work.

28 WEDNESDAY ☿ *Moon Age Day 21   Moon Sign Leo*

You can now make progress on home improvement projects and find ways to make yourself feel more settled and happy in your surroundings. You have good insight when it comes to your working life and you will already have one eye on the end of the year – a time at which certain of your plans come to fruition.

29 THURSDAY ☿ *Moon Age Day 22   Moon Sign Leo*

You are now entering a phase of radical alteration to both your ideas and your actions. Nothing much is likely to happen today but you are putting new ideas into place and your mind is going down paths you probably have not explored before. Every small step you take leads you to newer and more exciting places.

30 FRIDAY   ☿   *Moon Age Day 23   Moon Sign Virgo*

It might be said that Capricorn is now even more in tune with its own feelings than it has probably been for the last month or two. You should be fairly satisfied with the way things are going in a general sense, though you may decide that there isn't enough variety in your social life. If you make changes, take others into account.

December
2018

1 SATURDAY ☿ *Moon Age Day 24   Moon Sign Virgo*

Although you want to push on in a general sense you will probably have to be more aware of your own limitations today and that could mean having to rely on the good offices of those around you to a much greater extent than you normally would. There is a slight danger that you could allow your imagination to run away with you.

2 SUNDAY ☿ *Moon Age Day 25   Moon Sign Libra*

You now need a domestic atmosphere that is both warm and secure – a response to the present position of the Sun in your chart. There should be plenty of opportunity to relax and a great desire on your part to be kind to family members and friends. It looks as though you already have that Christmas spirit ahead of time.

3 MONDAY ☿ *Moon Age Day 26   Moon Sign Libra*

The desires of others could clash somewhat with your own needs and wants today and that might lead to a dispute or two. If so you can be fairly sure of getting your own way because you are extremely persuasive right now. Work issues could seem like heavy demands but other areas will be less stressed.

4 TUESDAY ☿ *Moon Age Day 27   Moon Sign Scorpio*

What a good time this would be for showing off and for convincing others that you are equal to just about any task they want to set you. From a social point of view you love places of entertainment and should willingly join in with pre-Christmas gatherings such as carol concerts or the local school Nativity play.

5 WEDNESDAY ☿ *Moon Age Day 28   Moon Sign Scorpio*

Home is a great place for entertaining at the moment and there is little doubt that you will be happier there than anywhere else. You may not have quite the level of drive that was evident a week or two ago but you are a great host right now and have what it takes to make everyone feel at ease. Your popularity is running very high.

6 THURSDAY ☿ *Moon Age Day 29   Moon Sign Scorpio*

This can be quite an exciting time romantically. Many Capricorns will already be getting into the mood for a holiday and there is likely to be some excitement around in the build-up to the Christmas period. You can also expect recognition of your talent today and an interest in many of your ideas, even the outrageous ones.

7 FRIDAY *Moon Age Day 0   Moon Sign Sagittarius*

You could encounter a little conflict with people in authority today. You are not in a mood to listen to what you think is nonsense and you are likely to say so, no matter who you are dealing with. Take care that you don't do or say something that could lead to you cutting off your nose to spite your face.

8 SATURDAY *Moon Age Day 1   Moon Sign Sagittarius*

This is a day when you will want to relax a little and improve your surroundings. Although you might be committed to work during the day, once the responsibilities are out of the way you will be spending some time planning for the future. This is one of Capricorn's favourite pastimes so you should be quite happy.

9 SUNDAY *Moon Age Day 2   Moon Sign Capricorn*

Generally speaking you should be in for a good time today and tomorrow. The lunar high finds you on top form and anxious to enjoy yourself, no matter what you happen to be doing. Put your best foot forward and do all that is necessary to make life better and easier. Finances are likely to be stronger than they have been for quite a while.

10 MONDAY

Moon Age Day 3   Moon Sign Capricorn

This is a favourable time for luck and personal growth. In quite a few ways the world should be opening up to you and the chance of you gaining ground at work especially is particularly strong. There are new gifts and blessings likely to be on the way and some of them come in such a disguised form it takes a while to recognise them.

11 TUESDAY

Moon Age Day 4   Moon Sign Aquarius

When it comes to the more personal side of your life, you could be going through something of a quiet revolution at the moment. You are looking very deeply at attachments and the way you have been responding to them. Changes may have to be made but these are all likely to be for the better in the end.

12 WEDNESDAY

Moon Age Day 5   Moon Sign Aquarius

Working within a team environment should suit you no end today. You have lots to offer and will be more co-operative than usual. There are times when Capricorn wants to be in charge and this can sometimes lead to conflict. For the moment you will be quite happy to brainstorm with almost anyone and you will relish the results.

13 THURSDAY

Moon Age Day 6   Moon Sign Aquarius

There is now less pressure about than could have been the case yesterday and you are more likely to drop back into an easy-going phase. The rest of the month is going to offer some very comfortable periods and times when you are focused equally on the past and the future. For today at least, the present is your best resort.

14 FRIDAY

Moon Age Day 7   Moon Sign Pisces

Opportunities that arise today are likely to take you in completely new directions. Although you have masses of energy and can get a great deal done, in the main you won't need to push yourself too hard. Lady Luck smiles on you and this makes it easy for you to achieve your objectives without too much effort.

15 SATURDAY *Moon Age Day 8   Moon Sign Pisces*

Your relaxed and sociable attitude during this part of December is likely to be very infectious. You may be starting the Christmas round already and probably socialising with colleagues and friends alike. This is a good time for low-key networking and for coming up with new schemes that can be played out after Christmas.

16 SUNDAY *Moon Age Day 9   Moon Sign Pisces*

Try to be as laid back as you can about domestic arrangements because everything seems to be running quite smoothly. If you are particularly nervous about something you have arranged, go over the details with a friend and then you can relax. In company you are charming, your nature is well balanced and you shine.

17 MONDAY *Moon Age Day 10   Moon Sign Aries*

At work you will probably still be very busy. If you are retired or between jobs at the moment you will be equally busy at home. Plans go ahead for new social encounters and there is plenty to get done across the next few days. In some ways you might discover that you are too active for your own good. Slow down a little.

18 TUESDAY *Moon Age Day 11   Moon Sign Aries*

High spirits continue to prevail and you can be the life and soul of any party – some of which you are quite happy to be organising. You have a strong impact on others and usually for their good but you can be just a little bossy when you come across situations you think are pointless or stupid. Try to be understanding today.

19 WEDNESDAY *Moon Age Day 12   Moon Sign Taurus*

Though your ego is quite strong today, you turn this to your advantage. There is no likelihood of you taking a back seat in anything during today and if there are new games to be played, you will definitely want to win. Split the day between family members and friends but don't try to do more than is sensible.

20 THURSDAY   *Moon Age Day 13   Moon Sign Taurus*

It might feel as though something about today is missing. Maybe you have forgotten to get in touch with someone or it could be that a particular friend has not been around recently. A little careful thought should put matters right and since you are especially good at organising today, get your sleeves rolled up.

21 FRIDAY   *Moon Age Day 14   Moon Sign Gemini*

Involvements in the social and romantic arena ought to prove rewarding now. Get out and meet others and try as many new things as you can. It's time for you to generally show off because you have much that others find attractive. What's more you will happily enjoy the limelight at present, without feeling in the least conspicuous.

22 SATURDAY   *Moon Age Day 15   Moon Sign Gemini*

Loved ones and all social connections prove to be important right now and with Christmas up ahead you may suddenly realise how many things you haven't done. That doesn't matter. What counts today is realising how much love surrounds you and making the most of it. You will be on good form socially towards the end of the day.

23 SUNDAY   *Moon Age Day 16   Moon Sign Cancer*

Stand by for a slightly sluggish period now that the lunar low has arrived. Look at this as a good thing as you will get it out of the way before Christmas actually arrives. You will need to rely a lot today on the good offices of others and if there is something you simply cannot do you will need to enlist the support of a professional.

24 MONDAY   *Moon Age Day 17   Moon Sign Cancer*

This is not the most suitable time to tempt fate by taking on risky propositions. Keep life steady and stick to what you know best. Grandiose schemes should wait until after today, by which time you will have forgotten about them anyway. Friends should prove to be loyal and supportive, and may want to draw you into everything.

25 TUESDAY   *Moon Age Day 18   Moon Sign Leo*

This is likely to be a romantic Christmas Day for many Capricorns. Your commitment to that someone special is particularly strong but you have more than enough affection to share out amongst family members and friends. There could be gifts on the way that you certainly never expected to get.

26 WEDNESDAY   *Moon Age Day 19   Moon Sign Leo*

Family and domestic matters are probably more rewarding today than they have been since the start of the Christmas holidays. There may be less incentive around to be on the go and there are gains to be made from staying in one place for a while and talking to family members. Plans for future journeys could easily be laid down today.

27 THURSDAY   *Moon Age Day 20   Moon Sign Virgo*

You could have to do a lot of rushing around today because it is just possible you are trying to balance a busy period at work with a much-enhanced social life. Romance is also centre stage at this time and you might be reappraising your approach to someone you fancy. You have a very positive attitude generally.

28 FRIDAY   *Moon Age Day 21   Moon Sign Virgo*

With significant changes coming along in your attitude – especially with regard to practicalities, you are quite inspirational in your thinking and actions today. At the same time you will want to indulge your fancies somewhat and will probably choose to spend time in the company of people you find to be intelligent and inspirational.

29 SATURDAY   *Moon Age Day 22   Moon Sign Libra*

You have a strong desire to expand your boundaries today and may already be tiring of all the parties and especially the mince pies. You want to get yourself back into gear but that won't be entirely possible until after the end of the year. For the moment, plan and keep yourself busy with social events.

30 SUNDAY
Moon Age Day 23   Moon Sign Libra

This can be a relaxed time of imaginative meditation, healing and spiritual renewal. Strong ideas are working their way to the surface all the time and issues that seemed complicated only a day or two ago can now be quite easy to deal with. This is also a time when you may be doing all you can to help those who are less fortunate than yourself.

31 MONDAY
Moon Age Day 24   Moon Sign Libra

Look out for a high-spirited period when you are certainly going to be very popular. What better trends could anyone want for this particular day of the year? You might not feel very much like working today but when it comes to enjoying yourself the sky is the limit. You will be as bright as the fireworks tonight and just as wonderful.

CAPRICORN:
2019 DIARY PAGES

CAPRICORN:
YOUR YEAR IN BRIEF

Capricorn relishes the fresh start of New Year's Day. As 2019 dawns you will be keen to get going and January and February offer you the perfect circumstances in which to do so. You will be making great strides in your career and in your relationship, too. Money matters will be variable but improving and your long-term plans may result in a significant success.

In a general sense you grow more comfortable as the spring begins to show itself in the hedgerows because you relish the changing year and all that it offers. Exercise is highlighted during March and April, with the accent now on waking from your winter sleep and getting to grips with practical matters. Money matters look particularly good towards the end of March and you will make the most of any unexpected gains.

May and June are good for consolidating your general position and for reaping some financial rewards, possibly as a result of efforts you have put in previously. With the warmer weather and the summer comes an urge to be on the move and a continuation of the restlessness that keeps returning this year. You should find that you can get others to follow your lead. You may not think yourself to be a natural leader but others may see you in that way.

With July and August comes an especially fortunate period. With a strong desire for change you could be travelling a lot, even if the journeys you take are only short in distance. You revel in new opportunities and will spend as much of your time out of doors as you can, especially in a sporting arena.

As the summer draws to a close you come into your own. September and October represent the two months that really work for you in almost every way, in particular the first half of October. With some effort, your love life could take a turn for the better. Money may come from unexpected directions and you will use some of this to further your plans.

With the end of the year comes an extra series of incentives and a push towards finishing those tasks that you set yourself much earlier in the year. It looks as though both November and December are going to be very busy for most Capricorns and there won't be as much time as you would wish for Christmas preparations. When it comes to enjoyment you won't have any trouble making the last part of December special. You finish the year with a real flourish and that is what counts.

January 2019

1 TUESDAY
Moon Age Day 25   Moon Sign Scorpio

You probably want a little peace and quiet on this New Year's Day, although finding it isn't likely to be all that easy. Later in the day you could learn something that will be to your advantage, but you will need to take care not to give offence, particularly when all you are trying to do is to help.

2 WEDNESDAY
Moon Age Day 26   Moon Sign Scorpio

Owing to higher levels of physical energy today, it is clear that you are more willing to be out there at the front. Any form of sporting activity is well highlighted, and you won't even mind being put on the spot in social situations under present trends. Your creative potential is also looking very good.

3 THURSDAY
Moon Age Day 27   Moon Sign Sagittarius

Be bold, brave and even foolhardy if you know it is going to get you what you want from life. You have the opportunity to excel in something you enjoy and shouldn't turn away from it, even if not everyone agrees. Disregard the opinion of anyone who is more focused on their own interests than yours.

4 FRIDAY
Moon Age Day 28   Moon Sign Sagittarius

Keep away from the sort of people who have a history of failure and disaster behind them, particularly if they are asking you for money. All in all, this is a time to keep your purse or wallet tightly closed. If you have to sign any documents at the moment, it would be good to read the small print very carefully indeed.

5 SATURDAY *Moon Age Day 0   Moon Sign Capricorn*

Start the weekend as you mean to go on, even if you don't feel exactly on top form as the day gets going. Later on though, the situation changes as the Moon grows ever closer to your own zodiac sign. By the evening, you might be feeling ready to paint the town red, or at least a deep shade of pink.

6 SUNDAY *Moon Age Day 1   Moon Sign Capricorn*

The lunar high brings you to a situation that simply demands that you throw yourself into it. There are ways to save money today while still enjoying yourself. Offer the sort of commitment to friends that you know they deserve, and be prepared for the rush of popularity that comes your way as a result.

7 MONDAY *Moon Age Day 2   Moon Sign Capricorn*

Someone is inclined to take the wind out of your sails, not because they are doing anything to upset you, but because they make it obvious how important you are to them. Whatever you take on today, it's important to aim for the top and not to allow distractions to get in the way.

8 TUESDAY *Moon Age Day 3   Moon Sign Aquarius*

There are some exciting and interesting possibilities in store for you at present. Look around you and see where the river of life wants to take you, because you can get much of what you want without having to try very hard right now. Convictions are important today, but don't take them to extremes.

9 WEDNESDAY *Moon Age Day 4   Moon Sign Aquarius*

There are some strong supporting elements around now and you can make use of them. The fact is that one or two people think a great deal of you, and are willing to say so in public situations. Be willing to stand up for someone who is in trouble, even if you have to put yourself out significantly to do so.

10 THURSDAY   *Moon Age Day 5   Moon Sign Pisces*

Good progress is still possible, although it might be somewhat restricted by a slightly negative attitude on your part if you are mixing with people who seem reluctant to give their all to situations. Be careful who you ally yourself with right now and, if possible, stick with those who you know to be successful.

11 FRIDAY   *Moon Age Day 6   Moon Sign Pisces*

Your confidence will be lacking in projects you don't understand, and for this reason it would be sensible for the moment to stick to some good old favourites. You are enjoying your creative mood, especially around the home, and could extend this to new hobbies or pastimes of your own.

12 SATURDAY   *Moon Age Day 7   Moon Sign Pisces*

A review of your life now leads to certain changes that you want to make. Don't be afraid to adopt an 'off with the old and on with the new' attitude, even if you find that this means a good deal of upheaval. This year inevitably brings changes into your life in any case, so you may as well be in charge of them.

13 SUNDAY   *Moon Age Day 8   Moon Sign Aries*

The trouble with today is that there are a host of things to do but perhaps not enough time to fit everything in. That's where planning is important. It is definitely better right now to do one task well rather than botch half a dozen. If the weather is fair, a good walk would almost certainly do you good.

14 MONDAY   *Moon Age Day 9   Moon Sign Aries*

Romance and personal relationships represent the area of life that might appeal the most right now. In a practical sense, there isn't too much you can do to make a splash, but looking ahead and planning isn't going to be a waste of time. What would really suit you down to the ground would be a change of scene.

15 TUESDAY *Moon Age Day 10   Moon Sign Taurus*

Although it might sometimes appear that the progress you make is limited, nothing could be further from the truth. You have a very positive attitude, especially at work, and might be singled out for some significant attention from superiors. Extra responsibilities are not out of the question.

16 WEDNESDAY *Moon Age Day 11   Moon Sign Taurus*

Domestic harmony should prevail now, leaving you with more hours to think about practical and professional matters. Rely on colleagues as much as you can because it is unlikely they will let you down at this time. Arrangements for meetings need to be made as early in the day as possible.

17 THURSDAY *Moon Age Day 12   Moon Sign Taurus*

This is a slightly up and down period and a time when you need to address the needs that your partner and possibly family members have of you. Avoid arguments but be prepared for some stimulating discussions. Puzzles of any sort suit your present frame of mind and could take up an hour or two later in the day.

18 FRIDAY *Moon Age Day 13   Moon Sign Gemini*

You are now eager to please and want to be liked by everyone. The slightly stubborn qualities of your zodiac sign are presently on hold and this makes you even nicer to know. It is not surprising therefore that you discover your popularity rating going right off the scale this Friday.

19 SATURDAY *Moon Age Day 14   Moon Sign Gemini*

A few blocks to your progress become evident but such is the nature of Capricorn that you simply concentrate your effort in directions your intuition tells you can pay dividends, There are one or two individuals coming into your life around this time who are going to have a very potent bearing on your future.

20 SUNDAY   *Moon Age Day 15   Moon Sign Cancer*

If there is one thing that is bound to get on your nerves at present, it is others telling you how you ought to live your life. Unfortunately, you don't have much option but to listen. The lunar low prevents you from pushing ahead by yourself and so you genuinely need to take the support that those around you can offer.

21 MONDAY   *Moon Age Day 16   Moon Sign Cancer*

The lunar low continues, and might put something of a dampener on spontaneous plans for outings or social gatherings. You can make things work out well for yourself but the amount of effort you have to put in could be so great that it taxes you too much. Bide your time until tomorrow, when trends change significantly.

22 TUESDAY   *Moon Age Day 17   Moon Sign Leo*

Look out for increased opportunities for romance. If you are in a settled relationship, things should be running smoothly and with some added excitement, while Capricorns who have been looking for love should certainly keep their eyes open today. You won't miss a trick when it comes to getting on well financially.

23 WEDNESDAY   *Moon Age Day 18   Moon Sign Leo*

You have a great deal of personal magnetism today and can exploit it in a number of different ways. If you want to get on well at work, turn on the charm there, though you might find the best use of your present influence will be socially and in a romantic sense. Few can refuse you your own way now.

24 THURSDAY   *Moon Age Day 19   Moon Sign Virgo*

Romance is most important now but thinking about it could cause you to miss one or two practical opportunities. That doesn't matter because you are committed to letting someone very special know how important they are to your life as a whole. Avoid getting tied down to pointless routines.

25 FRIDAY
Moon Age Day 20   Moon Sign Virgo

You want to enjoy life but for you that can mean work rather than play. There isn't a zodiac sign that toils away harder than you, not simply to feather your own nest but because you appreciate a job well done. However, you do need relaxation too, a fact you should address later in the day.

26 SATURDAY
Moon Age Day 21   Moon Sign Libra

You might need to clear the air regarding a personal matter and this in turn could mean that you divulge something deeply personal about yourself. Take heart from the fact that you should find a listening ear rather than one that ridicules you. Capricorn doesn't always reveal its innermost feeling but when it does they are appreciated.

27 SUNDAY
Moon Age Day 22   Moon Sign Libra

You are capable of working extremely hard at the moment and can get more or less anything you really want from life. However, all work and no play can make Capricorn extremely dull, something you particularly wish to avoid around now. Don't get bogged down with pointless jobs that have no real value.

28 MONDAY
Moon Age Day 23   Moon Sign Scorpio

Domestic issues might not be working out so well today but if you want to avoid getting bogged down with them, do something different. Of course, this doesn't mean ignoring your family but rather viewing them from a different perspective. An outing of some kind might do the trick.

29 TUESDAY
Moon Age Day 24   Moon Sign Scorpio

Today's chart indicates that emotions will be rising to the surface, particularly at home. You may want to avoid this and so will prefer to spend time with colleagues or casual friends who have no emotional draw on you. By the evening you will be quite happy to sit and watch the television.

30 WEDNESDAY *Moon Age Day 25   Moon Sign Sagittarius*

This is a day during which you should avoid getting on the wrong side of anyone at all. Assume nothing and check all details as carefully as you can. Most important of all, don't be argumentative over issues that have no real importance. The lighter your touch today, the greater the potential success.

31 THURSDAY *Moon Age Day 26   Moon Sign Sagittarius*

Creative efforts suit you especially well on this particular day, probably in the company of people you really like. This doesn't necessarily mean family members because you need the stimulus that comes from outside influences now. Maybe it's time to get in touch with someone you don't see very often.

February

2019

1 FRIDAY
Moon Age Day 27   Moon Sign Sagittarius

February is well and truly here and the call of the spring, though still some way off, doesn't escape your attention. You feel a pressing need to get out of doors, even if it is only for a brisk walk. At work, you might find some opposition building up to plans that are dear to your heart.

2 SATURDAY
Moon Age Day 28   Moon Sign Capricorn

As the weekend arrives, so the Moon moves into your own zodiac sign. It's time to get moving and there is very little at the moment that would be likely to hold you back. Keep a sense of proportion, but at the same time show a willingness to take the sort of risks that can get you ahead of the field.

3 SUNDAY
Moon Age Day 29   Moon Sign Capricorn

There are times to take a back seat and moments in your life when you have to push to the head of the queue. Today is a period when you can't afford to accept second best in any situation. Your plans should receive plenty of support and you should be enjoying a great deal of personal popularity. In a social sense you should make the most of it.

4 MONDAY
Moon Age Day 0   Moon Sign Aquarius

Financially speaking, prepare for a few ups and downs at this time. All the more reason to spend wisely and after due consideration. This is a good time for romantic encounters, and especially so for Capricorns who are not tied down to a committed relationship. Others find you intriguing now.

5 TUESDAY · · · · · · · · · *Moon Age Day 1 · Moon Sign Aquarius*

Your confidence grows gradually, but certainly isn't at a height today. You may decide that the time is right to do some planning and to look ahead of yourself in practical issues. This is not really a day for taking risks, though this is likely to change in the days ahead. Make the most of the evening.

6 WEDNESDAY · · · · · · *Moon Age Day 2 · Moon Sign Aquarius*

Full of character and enjoying some popularity now, this is the right time to go for what you want. Few people would refuse you at present, and your charm can bring anyone awkward around in a flash. Conforming to expectations is boring to you now and you love to surprise people.

7 THURSDAY · · · · · · · · · *Moon Age Day 3 · Moon Sign Pisces*

This has the potential to be an excellent day, with surprises coming like bolts from the blue and most of them favouring your own endeavours. You love to solve mysteries at present and will go to almost any length to uncover the truth. The people that matter are quite clearly on your side for the moment.

8 FRIDAY · · · · · · · · · · · · *Moon Age Day 4 · Moon Sign Pisces*

Retrieving what you can from difficult situations, you make the best of everything today and won't be let down by the actions of your friends, one or two of whom prove to be extremely supportive. Create a friendly atmosphere whenever you can and be willing to put yourself out, even for a stranger.

9 SATURDAY · · · · · · · · · · · *Moon Age Day 5 · Moon Sign Aries*

Your confidence remains paramount for much of the weekend, though you might find one or two problems coming from the direction of family members. If this turns out to be the case, solve them as early in the day as you can. After that, you will feel the need for a change of scene and for social diversity.

10 SUNDAY *Moon Age Day 6   Moon Sign Aries*

Rules and regulations are necessary, and you are not against inventing a few yourself on occasions. However, you don't always follow them and it certainly appears that you will not be doing so at the moment. There is an impish quality to your nature that allows you to find humour in any situation, professional, personal or social.

11 MONDAY *Moon Age Day 7   Moon Sign Aries*

You still seem to be working well, but you need to be aware that not everyone around you is working to your advantage. Keep an open mind about friends who call on your support. Though you might think one or two of them have been foolish, you can still be prevailed upon to help them out.

12 TUESDAY *Moon Age Day 8   Moon Sign Taurus*

Capricorn is on fine form at this stage of the week, particularly in a romantic sense. Be prepared to sweep someone off their feet and don't be against a little harmless flirting, no matter what your marital state. It does you good now and again to realise that you are more than attractive to some people.

13 WEDNESDAY *Moon Age Day 9   Moon Sign Taurus*

There are advantages about if you know where to look for them. Contrary to your previous thoughts, things are turning your way financially, whilst the social scene should look extremely interesting at this time. When it comes to impressing those around you, actions speak louder than words.

14 THURSDAY *Moon Age Day 10   Moon Sign Gemini*

Give yourself a pat on the back for something you have recently achieved, but don't become complacent. In most situations, there is still a long way to go and you haven't squeezed the best out of professional possibilities. Get a move on and avoid the slightly lethargic tendencies to which Capricorn is sometimes subject.

15 FRIDAY   *Moon Age Day 11   Moon Sign Gemini*

Friday brings a change of pace. In spheres of your life where things have been quiet, they now speed up, while in professional matters, there is a decline. Make the most of what life offers and be sure to show your partner how important they are to you. Changes to your home surroundings may seem interesting now.

16 SATURDAY   *Moon Age Day 12   Moon Sign Cancer*

Everything slows down as the lunar low comes along. You will need to spend some time thinking and will probably be happy to be on your own for much of the day. If this isn't possible, people are going to find you quieter than of late and you may have to explain why this is the case.

17 SUNDAY   *Moon Age Day 13   Moon Sign Cancer*

This may not be the most exciting Sunday you will even know, but it can be fairly solid all the same. Don't try anything too outrageous and if you have to work, follow the lead of people who are in the know. Keep your ideas to yourself for today, but be prepared to put them into practice soon.

18 MONDAY   *Moon Age Day 14   Moon Sign Leo*

Some of your most important plans might receive a shot in the arm now so it's good to pay attention to what's going on. However, there is also the slight possibility of some unrealistic expectations on your part, which although unusual for Capricorn is down to the present planetary line-up. Bide your time and ride out the trend.

19 TUESDAY   *Moon Age Day 15   Moon Sign Leo*

Your ego is now very strong, which could also make you rather more sensitive than would usually be the case. Ignore any slightly sarcastic comments from certain people that seem aimed at you, particularly because they probably come from jealousy rather than from genuine observation.

20 WEDNESDAY *Moon Age Day 16   Moon Sign Virgo*

Don't expect it to be easy to get exactly what you want from others or from life as a whole today. If you are too blasé the result will be more than a little frustration. Don't direct this at others and do your best to realise that these are very temporary trends. By as early as tomorrow you can turn situations around.

21 THURSDAY *Moon Age Day 17   Moon Sign Virgo*

This would be a very good period for working in conjunction with others on practical projects. A great deal of helpful input is on the way and you only have to listen to what family members and friends are saying in order to benefit from it. It would be advisable not to assume you have all the answers yourself.

22 FRIDAY *Moon Age Day 18   Moon Sign Libra*

You will probably want to please yourself today and might be going through a slightly lazy interlude. These come along now and again for Capricorn and as a result you might seek out a little luxury at some time during the day. Since you are usually on the go there is no harm in treating yourself now and again.

23 SATURDAY *Moon Age Day 19   Moon Sign Libra*

It seems that you have lessons to learn in the area of romance today. Perhaps you haven't been quite as attentive as you should or it is possible that the practical necessities of life have prevented you from spending as much time with your loved one as you would have wished. Now you can put things right.

24 SUNDAY *Moon Age Day 20   Moon Sign Scorpio*

Progress, whilst smooth enough, might seem somewhat slow but that won't really matter if you are simply chasing a good time. Social trends are good so that even if you are a Capricorn who works at the weekend there ought to be a few hours during the day to be with people you like to enjoy having small adventures with.

25 MONDAY   *Moon Age Day 21   Moon Sign Scorpio*

You are full of your own ego under these trends and your most important intention is to have fun. This might not be too easy to engineer at the start of the working week. However, with extra effort you can turn the most mundane situations into ones that please both yourself and those around you.

26 TUESDAY   *Moon Age Day 22   Moon Sign Sagittarius*

The focus is now likely to be on leisure and on the state of your love life. You will have the confidence to do the right things but could be deliberately delaying action in some cases. You may choose to have a restful day but it is more likely that things simply turn out that way. Enjoy the ride because life can be fun now.

27 WEDNESDAY *Moon Age Day 23   Moon Sign Sagittarius*

A short trip to see friends might be all that is needed to reassure you that they are doing well enough. Some Capricorns could be taking a short holiday at the moment and though it is still very early in the year, you could gain from travelling simply to have some fun. Routines could appear somewhat tedious.

28 THURSDAY *Moon Age Day 24   Moon Sign Sagittarius*

You have mental energy in abundance at present, together with a desire to solve puzzles of one sort or another. These need not be taken from a book but probably relate to life itself. Getting to grips with a situation at work could find you consulting a number of different but useful people.

March 2019

1 FRIDAY
Moon Age Day 25   Moon Sign Capricorn

Now that the lunar high is around again it comes as second nature to act on impulse. This is the time of the month when you will be actively seeking the chance to make an impression. You can afford to be fairly generous, both with your money and your time, and you make a big splash when it comes to social gatherings.

2 SATURDAY
Moon Age Day 26   Moon Sign Capricorn

Speak your mind today, and expect everyone to give you their full attention. You can't have everything you want from life at present, though you can come quite close. Lady Luck should be with you so it's worth investing your time in what you know to be a good idea, especially if you thought it up for yourself.

3 SUNDAY
Moon Age Day 27   Moon Sign Aquarius

There are a few possible gains to be made today, some of which may come as a surprise. This means you have to be ready for almost anything. Your powers of communication are good at present and you can really make an impression when it counts the most. Don't be too quick to judge the wisdom of friends.

4 MONDAY
Moon Age Day 28   Moon Sign Aquarius

Make this a Monday to remember. With spring now beginning to show in the hedgerows, and lighter nights more evident, it is quite likely that you will want to get out more. Today offers the perfect opportunity, probably in the company of people you always find entertaining.

5 TUESDAY   *Moon Age Day 29   Moon Sign Aquarius*

Not everything you do today is geared towards personal achievement. You are very sympathetic to the needs and wants of those around you and tend to spend a good deal of time listening to what others have to say. This behaviour increases your popularity and stands you in good stead later on.

6 WEDNESDAY   ☿   *Moon Age Day 0   Moon Sign Pisces*

You are now inclined to let others see your emotional side, which may come as a surprise to certain people in your environment. You aren't really a cold fish at all, but there is a natural reserve about Capricorn than can sometimes make you appear that way. Nobody will be left in any doubt about your feelings at present.

7 THURSDAY   ☿   *Moon Age Day 1   Moon Sign Pisces*

This is a day during which you want to concentrate on matters that are of interest specifically to you. If you can take others along with you, then so much the better, but what is really important is your own sense of satisfaction. Things that are old, curious or somehow mysterious could have special appeal.

8 FRIDAY   ☿   *Moon Age Day 2   Moon Sign Aries*

No matter how hard you try today, it is unlikely that you can make everything work out exactly the way you would wish. There are a number of reasons for this, all of which can be overcome if you are willing to seek out and accept a little help. Going it alone is not to be recommended for the moment.

9 SATURDAY   ☿   *Moon Age Day 3   Moon Sign Aries*

Avoid getting involved in arguments today. Not only are most of them completely unnecessary but also you don't stand much chance of winning them either. Even if you feel you have scored a victory, it will be marginal to say the least. You don't have to agree with everyone, but neither do you have to deliberately disagree.

10 SUNDAY ☿ *Moon Age Day 4   Moon Sign Taurus*

Don't put off until tomorrow something you can perfectly well do today. Time seems to stretch like elastic, allowing you to get a lot done and yet still leave hours free for social time, or to spend with your partner. Those Capricorns who are not romantically attached should keep their eyes open now.

11 MONDAY ☿ *Moon Age Day 5   Moon Sign Taurus*

Although you are probably feeling generally good about life, it is unlikely that you can make the headway you would wish at present. There may be obstacles placed in your path, though few if any of them are being deliberately created. The secret is to push on regardless and to remain optimistic.

12 TUESDAY ☿ *Moon Age Day 6   Moon Sign Taurus*

The obligations you feel towards others could be something of a bind today, leading you to doing what you have to, rather than what you feel you should. This is a temporary situation because you are usually as helpful as can be. By the evening you may be quite happy to take a rest.

13 WEDNESDAY ☿ *Moon Age Day 7   Moon Sign Gemini*

Despite a tendency to be outspoken in matters of the heart, you should be able to create a pleasant atmosphere at home under present trends and might also extend this ability to your working environment. It has now become important to you to make others feel comfortable. Your kindness might even pay off with a little financial reward under certain circumstances.

14 THURSDAY ☿ *Moon Age Day 8   Moon Sign Gemini*

You are now more active in a social sense. This is partly a response to present astrological trends but is also down to the advancing year and slightly better weather. If it's fine you could decide on some sort of journey today, preferably in the company of people with whom you feel easy and comfortable.

15 FRIDAY   ☿   *Moon Age Day 9   Moon Sign Cancer*

It could seem as if you do nothing but wait today. Not to worry, the lunar low is around in any case, so you won't be able to move any mountains. You have time to think and the ability to organise your thoughts into patterns of behaviour that will be useful another day.

16 SATURDAY   ☿   *Moon Age Day 10   Moon Sign Cancer*

The practical side of your nature is very much in evidence, but unless you are really sure about what you are doing, leave any actions until later. This Saturday is best for planning, and for observing the way others do things. You need these periods of calm and quiet, in order to deal with the busier times that will crop up regularly this year.

17 SUNDAY   ☿   *Moon Age Day 11   Moon Sign Cancer*

It may well occur to you today that the middle of the month has arrived already, and there are still jobs waiting that you wanted to start a couple of weeks ago. That's fine, because you have good powers of concentration right now and a determination to see jobs through to the very end. Hard work is easy for you.

18 MONDAY   ☿   *Moon Age Day 12   Moon Sign Leo*

This is an excellent time for getting into the good books of people who really count. The focus looks most likely to be targeted towards professional matters, although most spheres of your life are assisted by present trends. Don't be shy if you need to put across a particular and unique point of view.

19 TUESDAY   ☿   *Moon Age Day 13   Moon Sign Leo*

You are presently keen to take the initiative in any situation and will make your mind up about matters whilst others are still sitting and thinking. This quality stands you in good stead and could lead to a stronger financial position before long. The attitude of friends might be puzzling and consequently a little probing is called for.

20 WEDNESDAY ☿   *Moon Age Day 14*   *Moon Sign Virgo*

Your gift at the moment is the intensity of your perception, especially when it comes to assessing others. Someone in your life is very believable and some people around you are likely to be taken in, but not Capricorn. Rely on your gut reaction as it is not likely to be far wrong under these trends.

21 THURSDAY ☿   *Moon Age Day 15*   *Moon Sign Virgo*

When it comes to getting ahead in a practical sense, you might find yourself somewhat out on a limb at the moment. That's no real problem because Capricorn is quite capable of going it alone if necessary. As you go busily about but in a quiet and introspective mood, others may not know how to take you – but don't let this worry you.

22 FRIDAY ☿   *Moon Age Day 16*   *Moon Sign Libra*

If you seem loaded down with responsibilities today you can rest assured that you will be up for challenge or two and that you won't buckle under the pressure. The last working day of the week for many Capricorns will probably prove to be the most important and potentially the most rewarding.

23 SATURDAY ☿   *Moon Age Day 17*   *Moon Sign Libra*

Interests that you share jointly with someone close are of special importance today and you will be co-operating well with your partner or family members in order to provide a sound financial base for the future. You might not entirely enjoy the process but you will feel happier with your lot by the end of the day. Some travel restrictions are indicated.

24 SUNDAY ☿   *Moon Age Day 18*   *Moon Sign Scorpio*

Meetings with others might inspire some great ideas today, even though trends suggest you might be in a slightly provocative mood. It should be possible to start to get along with those you haven't always liked in the past now, as you are in a position to assess the situation truthfully.

25 MONDAY ☿ *Moon Age Day 19 Moon Sign Scorpio*

In some ways this might feel like the 'forgotten day' because not all that much is happening. At least the interlude gives you time to think and allows you the moments you need to ensure that those closest to you know how important they are. Don't waste this opportunity to be kind to everyone.

26 TUESDAY ☿ *Moon Age Day 20 Moon Sign Sagittarius*

You can do especially well now in joint business affairs or simply planning changes in and around your home. With a greater commitment towards co-operation, together with an instinctive ability to say the right thing, this Tuesday could prove to be not only very rewarding but also extremely happy.

27 WEDNESDAY ☿ *Moon Age Day 21 Moon Sign Sagittarius*

You might be seeking adventure today and be especially interested in changing things on the romantic front. As the Moon moves towards your zodiac sign you begin to be more active and open. The really likeable side of your personality now begins to shine out.

28 THURSDAY ☿ *Moon Age Day 22 Moon Sign Capricorn*

The Moon enters your zodiac sign, promising a progressive interlude, both today and tomorrow. You get yourself into gear quickly and can address a whole host of issues that have not been looked at in detail for several weeks. Most importantly, you are sociable, talkative and keen to learn.

29 FRIDAY *Moon Age Day 23 Moon Sign Capricorn*

This can be an extremely entertaining and positive day. Picking from what seems like a whole variety of different possibilities, you tend to favour social projects above professional ones right now. Personal relationships ought to be working out especially well. Make this evening a time to remember.

30 SATURDAY   *Moon Age Day 24   Moon Sign Capricorn*

A general push towards greater success continues but you can't really take anything for granted today. This is a period during which you need to check and recheck all details before you commit yourself to any specific course of action. Avoid getting involved in pointless discussions or arguments.

31 SUNDAY   *Moon Age Day 25   Moon Sign Aquarius*

Set out to make a good impression on the world by simply showing how kind you can be. Today should be both steady and happy, allowing you to gain ground in a number of different ways. Trends suggest that later in the day you will be able to make significant progress when love is in the air.

April

2019

1 MONDAY
Moon Age Day 26   Moon Sign Aquarius

You may get a chance today to broaden your personal horizons and to get on with things that might have puzzled you previously. Friendships should be strong and people who have not played an important part in your life up to now start to become more significant. Look out for some unexpected financial gains.

2 TUESDAY
Moon Age Day 27   Moon Sign Pisces

Make this a day to think up new ideas. Positions in your chart indicate that anything devised now has the potential to bring significant advantages into your life with the fullness of time. There are some fairly unusual circumstances about, leading to many coincidences and strange happenings. Most of these seem geared towards your greater success.

3 WEDNESDAY
Moon Age Day 28   Moon Sign Pisces

You can't avoid the feeling that this is an 'off with the old and on with the new' time in your life generally. That's fine, but don't go too far just because you feel you are on a roll. It is just possible that you could abandon ways of thinking and acting that are not at all at fault in favour of ones that don't serve you as well.

4 THURSDAY
Moon Age Day 29   Moon Sign Pisces

Impressive socially, you find that events conspire to present you with enjoyable and stimulating company. Taking life in your stride, you should enjoy today and make a great deal of personal offers and invitations. When it comes to romance, you are in a good position to show your loved one exactly how you feel.

5 FRIDAY
Moon Age Day 0   Moon Sign Aries

You may feel that this is a less interesting period following the generally positive trends of yesterday, but while quieter it should still be successful. At work it would be sensible to avoid putting off until tomorrow what you can easily do today. You may bump into an old friend or contact.

6 SATURDAY
Moon Age Day 1   Moon Sign Aries

Take special care where emotional issues are at stake today. It's easy for others to misunderstand what you are saying and to jump to the wrong conclusion as a result. There are gains to be made through inventiveness and by being in the right place at the right time.

7 SUNDAY
Moon Age Day 2   Moon Sign Taurus

There is now much to be gained from broadening your personal horizons. Young Capricorns, or those looking for love, can expect opportunities to come along. Perhaps you have an admirer you would never have guessed at, or you might discover that a friend would wish to be very much more. The possibilities are endless.

8 MONDAY
Moon Age Day 3   Moon Sign Taurus

Expect to be streets ahead of others at work, or in any competitive endeavour. Don't fight shy of letting people know what you think. It is true that you are rather outspoken at the moment, but much of what you have to say makes a great deal of sense. Keep a sense of proportion regarding your spending.

9 TUESDAY
Moon Age Day 4   Moon Sign Gemini

Don't allow the views of others to influence your life to any great degree today. Of course, it is important to take on board alternative opinions, but that isn't the same as turning your world upside down to accommodate them. Remain interested and flexible, but only up to a point.

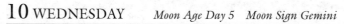

10 WEDNESDAY   *Moon Age Day 5   Moon Sign Gemini*

The planets now give you a lot of opportunity to make smooth progress. At work you should be able to address most matters well and are unlikely to back down over issues you think are important. Your personal life is likely to be settled, with romantic interludes permeating a generally sedate period.

11 THURSDAY   *Moon Age Day 6   Moon Sign Gemini*

A few emotional tensions can begin to surface now, leaving you feeling slightly wrung out. Although these have to be addressed, perhaps you don't have to take them quite as seriously as you might be inclined to do. People are generally on your side, even if it doesn't always appear that this is the case.

12 FRIDAY   *Moon Age Day 7   Moon Sign Cancer*

You are likely to prefer to take it easy today, so don't expect to be happy if you are faced with unavoidable obligations. The lunar low makes you somewhat lethargic and less than happy to push yourself physically. Routines suit you at the moment because there is great security in doing what you know and understand.

13 SATURDAY   *Moon Age Day 8   Moon Sign Cancer*

The planetary low patch continues and there really isn't much point in trying to alter the situation. To do so would be to knock your head against a brick wall. Simply sit and watch life go by, secure in the knowledge that, behind the scenes, the weekend offers many more opportunities than you might currently realise.

14 SUNDAY   *Moon Age Day 9   Moon Sign Leo*

The Moon moves on, and now when it comes to taking the initiative you won't be found in any way wanting on this Sunday. Take a close look around you. The summer is approaching fast, with the nights getting shorter and everything in the garden beginning to grow. Like the flowers, you need more space now.

15 MONDAY

Moon Age Day 10 *Moon Sign Leo*

Along comes a period when you will delight in the opportunity to get out and about. There are things to do and people to meet. The sociable side of your nature is more than evident and you take great delight in all sorts of company. Don't be surprised if you find yourself on the receiving end of someone's joke.

16 TUESDAY

Moon Age Day 11 *Moon Sign Virgo*

You now find yourself in the middle of an easy-going period and a time when those around you are more than willing to take at least part of the strain. Avoid a tendency to be too clever, even when you are dealing with subject matter that you understand only too well. Capricorn needs to be modest now.

17 WEDNESDAY

Moon Age Day 12 *Moon Sign Virgo*

Capricorn can be quite stubborn on occasions, particularly so if those around you seem to be behaving in a stupid or irresponsible manner. Nevertheless you will simply have to bite your tongue in order to avoid unpleasantness. There isn't really room for arguments right now, so stay cheerful instead.

18 THURSDAY

Moon Age Day 13 *Moon Sign Libra*

Stay away from crowded places or from situations in which you have no chance to prove your own worth. Standing in isolation gets you noticed much more right now, even though you do tend to feel slightly shy now and again. Luckily, this aspect of Capricorn is far less likely to show at present.

19 FRIDAY

Moon Age Day 14 *Moon Sign Libra*

This is another day during which you must stay away from disputes or arguments that can't have any sensible outcome. Settle for a steady sort of day and allow others to have their say. Your spirits will be higher as the hours wear on and you will also notice that some of the people you associate with are kinder.

20 SATURDAY *Moon Age Day 15 Moon Sign Scorpio*

If you have been working positively and deliberately towards a specific objective, today ought to see you able to win through. In a more personal sense you should find that romantic encounters with your loved one have much to offer. Even if not everyone sees things your way, your partner is likely to do so.

21 SUNDAY *Moon Age Day 16 Moon Sign Scorpio*

Trends highlight communications today. You should be getting on especially well with groups of friends or associates. It is likely that your sense of freedom is especially strong at present and you certainly will not take kindly to being restricted in any way. You may also become aware of the need others have of you.

22 MONDAY *Moon Age Day 17 Moon Sign Sagittarius*

In business matters you may benefit from a little luck coming your way soon, though it is likely to be of the sort that is lead by your actions. This might not seem to apply today but it is clear that something you do or say now is going to have a bearing on events later in the week.

23 TUESDAY *Moon Age Day 18 Moon Sign Sagittarius*

You are getting as much as you can from practical and career matters at present but are you really as happy as you should be? This might be a good time to take stock and to see if what you are doing is having the desired result in terms of your own needs. Some of your conclusions might be surprising.

24 WEDNESDAY *Moon Age Day 19 Moon Sign Capricorn*

With the arrival of the lunar high you ought to be feeling on top form so that, even when difficulties do arise, you are in an excellent position to deal with them instantly. Be willing to be a little flexible in your financial planning because there is natural good luck to be taken into account today.

25 THURSDAY   *Moon Age Day 20   Moon Sign Capricorn*

This is another excellent time for putting your luck to the test. Progressive decision-making is also possible, together with a strong sense of destiny regarding specific issues. Elements of the past have a bearing on the present so don't be surprised if there are a significant amount of coincidences cropping up now.

26 FRIDAY   *Moon Age Day 21   Moon Sign Capricorn*

This is a time during which you could benefit greatly from a greater understanding of life in general, especially if you have a particular interest in other cultures and philosophies. Capricorns taking a holiday or travelling on business around now are likely to get a great deal from the experience.

27 SATURDAY   *Moon Age Day 22   Moon Sign Aquarius*

Once again the planets line themselves up to show advantages through movement and travel. If circumstances prevent you from getting around in a physical sense, remember that allowing your mind to move can be just as good. An appealing book can take the sign of Capricorn almost as far as an aeroplane.

28 SUNDAY   *Moon Age Day 23   Moon Sign Aquarius*

Your relationship probably brings the greatest highlights now, particularly as you are inclined to open up to new ways of thinking about life. Sharing is important and, although it is something you don't always understand as much as you might, you realise now that your journey through life is meant to be a co-operative one.

29 MONDAY   *Moon Age Day 24   Moon Sign Pisces*

Look for people who can help you to expand your knowledge and understanding of certain matters. Travel and intellectual pursuits have much to offer you at this time and it isn't out of the question that some sons and daughters of Capricorn will have planned a particular journey for this period.

30 TUESDAY

Moon Age Day 25   Moon Sign Pisces

At work you will have plenty of enthusiasm to get your plans working properly. At the same time you ought to notice that those around you are taking more notice of what you are saying and the way you do things. It should be easy to influence others and this could lead to an interesting new relationship.

May

2019

1 WEDNESDAY
Moon Age Day 26   Moon Sign Pisces

You now enter a period that is ripe for joint financial ventures and for persuading those around you to follow a path you have chosen. Start Wednesday as you mean to go on, with plenty of positive action and a willingness to co-operate. Love can play an important part in your thinking at present.

2 THURSDAY
Moon Age Day 27   Moon Sign Aries

Capricorn enjoys some personal magnetism at the moment and so you should be able to make a really good impression on almost anyone you meet. There won't be all that much in the way of new opportunities though, unless of course you make them for yourself. Friendships should be positive.

3 FRIDAY
Moon Age Day 28   Moon Sign Aries

Your influence over everyday matters could feel somewhat restricted at this time so don't expect to be able to do as much as you would wish, at least for part of today. In the end it's up to you because extra effort is needed if you really want to get ahead. Curb any tendency to think you know everything.

4 SATURDAY
Moon Age Day 0   Moon Sign Taurus

Today's trends should prove to be mentally stimulating. Your understanding of certain issues is broadened and long-range travel trends look good. Perhaps you are planning for a holiday that is to come or it could be that your work is going to take you abroad. Even short journeys look good this weekend.

5 SUNDAY   *Moon Age Day 1   Moon Sign Taurus*

Freedom beckons and if there is something you are very keen on
at the moment it is feeling that the choices are yours. You certainly
will not take kindly to being told what to do by anyone and would
kick against anyone who did so. Neither will you be very pleased if
people take you for granted at any stage right now.

6 MONDAY   *Moon Age Day 2   Moon Sign Taurus*

Your spirit of independence rides high under present planetary
trends and you are very happy about it. Be bold and determined and
get what you want, but resist any temptation to bulldoze your ideas
through. Listen to the opinions of younger family members who
might be more in touch in certain areas than you are.

7 TUESDAY   *Moon Age Day 3   Moon Sign Gemini*

Though you are likely to enjoy activities that involve groups of
people you might be less happy on a one-to-one basis for today
at least. Keep it light and simple and don't expect too much from
anyone. The more matter-of-fact your own attitude is, the greater is
the sense of enjoyment that is likely to come your way.

8 WEDNESDAY   *Moon Age Day 4   Moon Sign Gemini*

This would be a good time to broaden your horizons significantly.
You are able to keep going physically for a long stretch just for today,
and your powers of concentration are second to none. Keep an open
mind about the behaviour of a particularly good friend. There might
be good reasons behind it.

9 THURSDAY   *Moon Age Day 5   Moon Sign Cancer*

Now the lunar low comes around, so it would be best to suspend
major activities for the moment and settle instead for a peaceful,
perhaps even idyllic, time in the company of people with whom you
feel particularly comfortable. Arrangements can be made for busier
times that are planned for early next week.

10 FRIDAY
Moon Age Day 6   Moon Sign Cancer

Any attempts to get ahead today are likely to meet with little major success. The problem is not you or your efforts but the position of the Moon at the moment. Suspend some of your activities until tomorrow, a time during which they are much more likely to bear fruit. For now, simply relax.

11 SATURDAY
Moon Age Day 7   Moon Sign Leo

Irritations could come along today from the direction of new friends or acquaintances. Try to stem your impatience with people who genuinely don't know you all that well and keep calm, even if you have to explain something ten times over. Avoid unnecessary complications as far as your love life is concerned.

12 SUNDAY
Moon Age Day 8   Moon Sign Leo

At work you are now very enterprising and will be anxious to show colleagues just how much you know. You may have one or two new ideas that you probably ought to keep to yourself for the moment, that is unless you want someone to steal them from under you. Don't be suspicious at the moment – just careful.

13 MONDAY
Moon Age Day 9   Moon Sign Virgo

It appears that you now enjoy greatly improved communication skills and that you will be turning these towards feathering your nest in a financial and also a social way. You show significant concern for others so there is no reason at all why you should not get on well yourself. Don't feel guilty or selfish.

14 TUESDAY
Moon Age Day 10   Moon Sign Virgo

Personal matters are to the forefront of your mind at the moment and you have what it takes to make today very special for the person you love the most. You are likely to be very chatty just now and will be at the forefront of any social gatherings that are taking place in your vicinity.

15 WEDNESDAY   *Moon Age Day 11   Moon Sign Libra*

You are now in a very good position to call the shots where future plans are concerned. What matters is that you are doing your homework, which others may not manage so well. This means your point of view is reasoned and difficult to fault. In business, you tend to be extremely shrewd at present.

16 THURSDAY   *Moon Age Day 12   Moon Sign Libra*

Casual contacts could be preferred today, rather than intense ones. Your present matter-of-fact attitude does not wish to be stifled by too much depth and practical matters are close to your heart right now. Don't be surprised if you find yourself taking a sudden and rather unexpected change in direction.

17 FRIDAY   *Moon Age Day 13   Moon Sign Scorpio*

You will have extra energy now, which is why you seem to be taking on so much new work. Once the responsibilities are out of the way you can turn your attention towards having a good time, something you are going to be especially attracted to both today and across the coming weekend. Give a friend a boost if they need one.

18 SATURDAY   *Moon Age Day 14   Moon Sign Scorpio*

A good deal of what happens now depends on the say-so of others. This is slightly frustrating because you may get a good deal of the way down a road of your own construction, only to find that you need some sort of permission to proceed. Try to remain patient and argue your case eloquently.

19 SUNDAY   *Moon Age Day 15   Moon Sign Scorpio*

This ought to be a fairly good time with regard to money. What you already have, you tend to hold on to, whilst the possibility of making more is never far away. Don't necessarily believe all you hear from others, even friends. People could be quite misinformed at the moment.

20 MONDAY   *Moon Age Day 16   Moon Sign Sagittarius*

Your ability to command attention and impress others can be put to the test today. With plenty going for you in a general sense and material situations still looking good, it's time to go for gold. Although not everyone appears to have your best interests at heart, when it matters most friends come up trumps.

21 TUESDAY   *Moon Age Day 17   Moon Sign Sagittarius*

Family matters should now be putting a smile on your face. Younger relatives especially have the ability to make you laugh, but so do many other situations and people because your sense of humour is so highly charged now. Plan for a different sort of time ahead, with the possibility of movement and travel.

22 WEDNESDAY   *Moon Age Day 18   Moon Sign Capricorn*

A mainly fortunate period comes along as the Moon moves into your zodiac sign. Although you could feel that you deserve more than you are getting from life, your ability to look ahead and to establish new contacts is what wins through in the end. This could be a very fortunate time for some limited speculation.

23 THURSDAY   *Moon Age Day 19   Moon Sign Capricorn*

Your powers of persuasion are good and it appears you can get most of what you want at the moment. The lunar high helps you to persuade others that yours in the right chosen path and you should discover new talents that you didn't even know you possessed. This should all lead to a positive start to a brand new interlude.

24 FRIDAY   *Moon Age Day 20   Moon Sign Aquarius*

The more widespread and different the company you find yourself in today, the better you are likely to feel. Abandoning for the moment thoughts of security and comfort, you may be seeking to put yourself to the test in a physical sense. Remember birthdays in the family and amongst your friends. This is a good emailing day.

25 SATURDAY   *Moon Age Day 21   Moon Sign Aquarius*

Your mind could turn towards creative pursuits of one sort or another. Yours is a very practical zodiac sign, so anything arty tends to have an everyday function for you too. Since you are an Earth sign, perhaps you might turn to something like pottery? There could also be some movement on the romantic front.

26 SUNDAY   *Moon Age Day 22   Moon Sign Aquarius*

It would be best to get your feelings out in the open today. Your zodiac sign has a tendency to bottle things up at times, which is very rarely the right way to proceed. You could experience some small difficulty with mechanical gadgets of one sort or another and might have to enlist some help.

27 MONDAY   *Moon Age Day 23   Moon Sign Pisces*

It could seem as though everyone else is getting ahead, leaving you at the starting post. But remember the story of the tortoise and the hare. Look around you today, do some thinking and spend time weighing up situations. When you do decide to start running, watch out world!

28 TUESDAY   *Moon Age Day 24   Moon Sign Pisces*

Today is definitely one of those times during which you get out of life almost exactly what you put into it. If you want to be lethargic, situations won't demand much of you, but you won't make the gains either. Better by far to go for gold and then to glory in the attention that comes your way.

29 WEDNESDAY   *Moon Age Day 25   Moon Sign Aries*

In a general sense, you are likely to be very high-spirited at present. This attitude is infectious, as you are about to find out. Your popularity remains high and might actually increase. All the attention coming your way at the moment is great, but it isn't what Capricorn usually looks for or expects.

30 THURSDAY
Moon Age Day 26   Moon Sign Aries

Address issues one at a time today and don't bite off more than you can chew. In the romantic department, it looks as though you are in for a very positive time. Those Capricorns who have been looking for love could have a great deal more success now than has been the case for some days past.

31 FRIDAY
Moon Age Day 27   Moon Sign Aries

Today should be fairly enjoyable but some of the glitter might be taken off social situations if the odd wet blanket comes along. Although there isn't really a great deal you can do to avoid this eventuality, you should be able to cheer up the most depressing of people with your present bubbly nature.

2019

1 SATURDAY
Moon Age Day 28   Moon Sign Taurus

Now you can make your move, both at home and in personal situations. To the outside world you look successful and impressive, which means you are probably at the peak of your powers. Even if you don't feel entirely sure of yourself, it's the impression you give that means the most.

2 SUNDAY
Moon Age Day 29   Moon Sign Taurus

Events in your career should be quite fulfilling, even though many Capricorns won't actually be working on a Sunday. If this is the case for you, use the time to plan for later – but don't spend all day doing so. People around you want to have some fun and the way you are feeling at present, you will want to join in.

3 MONDAY
Moon Age Day 0   Moon Sign Gemini

Good news could be coming in from a number of different directions, some of which prove to be quite surprising. This you will be taking in your stride and at the same time, you will be seeking change and diversity in your life. Don't be too surprised if you are being singled out for special treatment.

4 TUESDAY
Moon Age Day 1   Moon Sign Gemini

Most matters can go your way today, with just a little effort on your part. If there are celebrations in the family, or within your friendship circle, there's a good chance you will want to join in. You should have a fairly carefree attitude to life at present and can certainly enjoy all that romance offers.

107

5 WEDNESDAY

Moon Age Day 2   Moon Sign Cancer

Snap decisions are not wise while the lunar low is around, though surprisingly you tend to feel rather better about yourself and life today. For a number of planetary reasons you have faith in your own abilities and should be in a position to talk both fairly and rationally to those around you.

6 THURSDAY

Moon Age Day 3   Moon Sign Cancer

Avoid rash decisions or prohibitive actions for today and be willing to watch and wait. Your moment will come soon enough and if you recognise this, you will actively want to clear the decks for the action that lies ahead, particularly at work. As the day progresses, so your confidence grows and circumstances alter in your favour.

7 FRIDAY

Moon Age Day 4   Moon Sign Leo

The things you learn today can be turned to your own advantage, so it appears that in addition to having plenty to say for yourself, you are also keeping your ears open. Some Capricorns might get a chance at some real power, mainly in a career sense. Do as much work as you can today because tomorrow's trends will call for caution.

8 SATURDAY

Moon Age Day 5   Moon Sign Leo

Don't believe everything you hear today because the chances are someone is deliberately trying to get one over on you. Subject everything to the same level of Capricorn scrutiny and give some thought to testing out one or two of your big ideas before you put them into practice.

9 SUNDAY

Moon Age Day 6   Moon Sign Virgo

You appear to be in the middle of a generally beneficial period. What works best for you at the moment is talking. Capricorn is unusual, because it can be quite chatty or completely silent, it all depends on the day. For now, there is hardly a subject coming your way that you will fail to tell everyone all about.

10 MONDAY
Moon Age Day 7   Moon Sign Virgo

Friendship is high on your list of priorities today, even if you are busy in a practical sense for most of the time. When you do get a moment, don't forget to say thank you for someone's kindness and bear in mind the needs of people who are going through a hard time right now.

11 TUESDAY
Moon Age Day 8   Moon Sign Virgo

It is only if you try to do too much today that you will find yourself coming unstuck. The tried-and-tested Capricorn route to success is especially necessary under prevailing trends, and this is one job at a time, and every one undertaken to the very best of your ability. Slowly and surely, you achieve your objectives.

12 WEDNESDAY
Moon Age Day 9   Moon Sign Libra

Although many of your personal ambitions are now clearly on course, don't overstep the mark and expect too much, either of others or yourself. Tread carefully where finances are concerned, and certainly never push anyone into taking financial risks that might frighten them.

13 THURSDAY
Moon Age Day 10   Moon Sign Libra

There are chores galore today, or at least that is the way it looks. Don't be too surprised if you are a little down in the dumps, though it is clear that matters lie predominantly in your own hands. Your creative potential is good, but you could find obstacles being put in your path.

14 FRIDAY
Moon Age Day 11   Moon Sign Scorpio

Demands being made of you at work appear to be your main priority at the moment. Remember to take time out to enjoy yourself too. Don't be too quick to jump to conclusions, particularly when dealing with people you don't know all that well. You could be suffering from an over-suspicious nature today.

15 SATURDAY   *Moon Age Day 12   Moon Sign Scorpio*

Career developments may be aided by people who are in the know, though you won't want to waste a second of what the weekend has to offer romantically and socially. You are still riding high in the estimation of most people and are especially popular with those who see you as being a source of good advice.

16 SUNDAY   *Moon Age Day 13   Moon Sign Sagittarius*

You are instinctively friendly with just about everyone today, which is a positive fact for a number of different reasons. In addition to making others feel good, you might also end up helping yourself in ways you never intended. You should also find more in the way of general good luck coming along.

17 MONDAY   *Moon Age Day 14   Moon Sign Sagittarius*

You ought to be getting where you want to go in many senses now but especially with regard to work. Some positive things may come from some quite unexpected directions and bring you new opportunities too. Friends should prove to be both helpful and interested in what you have to say.

18 TUESDAY   *Moon Age Day 15   Moon Sign Capricorn*

You won't have to look too hard for good fortune today because the Moon should ensure it comes your way of its own accord. However, although you are lucky today, you are not invulnerable. In amongst all the positive action, spend at least a few moments thinking about your personal security.

19 WEDNESDAY   *Moon Age Day 16   Moon Sign Capricorn*

It won't be too difficult to get your own way now, even with people who are tougher to crack than nuts. The fact is that you are seen as being very likeable and a good deal more flexible than is sometimes the case for Capricorn. Acting on impulse is not really you, but it does seem to work at present.

20 THURSDAY   *Moon Age Day 17   Moon Sign Capricorn*

If you find yourself involved in dealings with those higher up the professional tree than you are, today should prove to be quite useful. The ability to make a good impression is highlighted, as is your tendency to make others laugh. The silly side of Capricorn might not show every day but it's well-marked now.

21 FRIDAY   *Moon Age Day 18   Moon Sign Aquarius*

Although your schedule might be somewhat overloaded, especially in a professional sense, you seem to enjoy the situation and can get a great deal done today. In any case, under prevailing trends it is quite possible that slowing down would prove to be a mistake. You are allowed to accept help, though.

22 SATURDAY   *Moon Age Day 19   Moon Sign Aquarius*

There may now be a need for some sort of renewal in your life. Although the year is pressing on this may be simply mean a spring clean of your thoughts and desires. If you feel tempted to take shortcuts towards some of your objectives, bear in mind that this would almost certainly be a mistake.

23 SUNDAY   *Moon Age Day 20   Moon Sign Pisces*

This may be one of the best days of the month, not only for being the centre of attention but for realising that this is the case. Taking things for granted at home is not to be recommended. Personal attachments represent one of the few areas of life that does need extra work at this time.

24 MONDAY   *Moon Age Day 21   Moon Sign Pisces*

There is at least one project in your life that now needs rethinking from scratch and you are not afraid to tackle it. Although this may be quite annoying at first, the fact that you are prepared to go to these lengths proves that you are very aware of present trends and the way you need to react to them. Getting things right second time is better than failing altogether.

25 TUESDAY
Moon Age Day 22   Moon Sign Pisces

Some delays are more or less inevitable today. If you are wise you will realise that this is not the best time for starting new projects or for trying to bulldoze your way towards chosen objectives. Take a day or two to think about things and whilst you are doing so, enjoy the positive domestic and personal trends.

26 WEDNESDAY
Moon Age Day 23   Moon Sign Aries

If it appears that others are making mountains out of molehills maybe you should tell them so, though as diplomatically as you know how. Being too direct is not going to help at all right now, so use all the tact you have at your disposal. This is especially true when dealing with professional superiors.

27 THURSDAY
Moon Age Day 24   Moon Sign Aries

Social concerns are clearly on your mind now and you are still inclined to over-worry about matters you probably can't control at all. Getting an early start can be quite important and then at least you will be ahead of the game. All friendships, including casual ones with acquaintances, may prove important today.

28 FRIDAY
Moon Age Day 25   Moon Sign Taurus

The smooth running of your everyday life could seem to be going slightly awry, which won't please you at all. What you do have at your disposal, however, is a very positive and active sense of humour. As long as you can laugh at yourself, you will also keep all matters in a sensible perspective.

29 SATURDAY
Moon Age Day 26   Moon Sign Taurus

Try to get yourself involved in projects today that need to be finished before you start others. Although multitasking is usually something you cope with well, this skill seems to be somewhat lacking right now. You will probably have more influence today with people who are especially important in your life.

30 SUNDAY
Moon Age Day 27   Moon Sign Gemini

You have a great chance to increase your circle of close friends this Sunday. Although you could make even more progress in a practical or even a professional sense, enough may be enough for the moment. Everyone needs to have fun now and again and it is your time this Sunday.

July

2019

1 MONDAY
Moon Age Day 28   Moon Sign Gemini

Although opportunities to get ahead are not legion, you will recognise them when they occur and will squeeze through any crack to get at them. Some people might accuse you of being sneaky and self-seeking, though the truth is that you also have the interests of relatives, friends and colleagues at heart.

2 TUESDAY
Moon Age Day 0   Moon Sign Gemini

There may be certain emotional pressures that you will have to work against today. Don't be too quick to push your point of view forward, particularly when you are talking to your partner or loved ones. While you don't lack confidence, you still can't be certain of bringing everyone on side now.

3 WEDNESDAY
Moon Age Day 1   Moon Sign Cancer

This is not a day during which significant progress is likely to be made. Instead, consolidate and wait patiently for matters to mature. In the meantime, do your best to enjoy yourself and spend more time doing those things that feel right in a social and personal sense.

4 THURSDAY
Moon Age Day 2   Moon Sign Cancer

Keeping expectations moderate is what matters now. Your confidence is low during the two days that the Moon is in your opposite sign, and pushing against the tide is unlikely to help matters. Remain chatty and confident if you can, planning carefully and looking towards greater movement later.

5 FRIDAY   *Moon Age Day 3   Moon Sign Leo*

A much more progressive and positive phase comes along, with better potential advancements at work and a more determined attitude on your part. People you have not mixed with for a while might be making a return to your life soon, though some of these might be people with whom you have argued previously.

6 SATURDAY   *Moon Age Day 4   Moon Sign Leo*

You can't trust to luck today, but rather your own abilities. It might also be a mistake to automatically believe what others are saying. You wouldn't suggest, or even believe, that people are lying. On the contrary, they might be as much in the dark as you are and merely quoting possibilities.

7 SUNDAY   *Moon Age Day 5   Moon Sign Virgo*

Along comes a socially helpful period, during which those around you are more willing than ever to put themselves out on your behalf. Don't be too quick to judge the actions or opinions of a friend, but stay flexible and even suggestible. Routines will bore you today, so avoid them.

8 MONDAY   ☿   *Moon Age Day 6   Moon Sign Virgo*

Teamwork and co-operative ventures probably have less to offer you at present than they have over the last couple of weeks. You are in a go-it-alone frame of mind and that means having to rely more and more on yourself. The situation is rather different in terms of personal attachments however.

9 TUESDAY   ☿   *Moon Age Day 7   Moon Sign Libra*

Along comes a more industrious period, spurred on by the Moon. Potential gains come from almost any sort of investment and it is just possible that a move you made some months ago is now really paying dividends. Listen to what good friends have to say about your social life. They could have a point.

10 WEDNESDAY ☿   *Moon Age Day 8   Moon Sign Libra*

This is a better time than most in which to keep your eyes and ears open for new chances of almost any sort. Your creative skills look especially good and you instinctively know what looks and feels right. Moving outside your usual social mainstream, you probably feel alive and ready to mix with anyone.

11 THURSDAY ☿   *Moon Age Day 9   Moon Sign Scorpio*

The demands of your life make little indulgences less than likely at the moment. Circumstances may conspire to force you into the limelight, a position you will not enjoy all that much. Don't be too quick to judge people or situations now and listen very carefully to the thoughts of your partner.

12 FRIDAY ☿   *Moon Age Day 10   Moon Sign Scorpio*

Don't be afraid to consider specific changes to your life if you know in your heart that they are going to benefit you later. Not everything goes your way today but you should be enjoying the summer and making the most of every opportunity to find fresh fields and pastures new.

13 SATURDAY ☿ *Moon Age Day 11   Moon Sign Sagittarius*

Confused situations will follow if you put your faith in the wrong people today. It might be better to follow your own conscience in most matters and to stay away from deliberately provocative types. None of this prevents you from enjoying a generally happy and quite eventful Saturday.

14 SUNDAY ☿ *Moon Age Day 12   Moon Sign Sagittarius*

It would be best to opt for some light relief today and that is what you should be thinking about. There are substantial gains to be made where friendship is concerned, and sociable associations with others could also lead to you discovering ways to get ahead in a financial as well as a personal way.

15 MONDAY ☿ *Moon Age Day 13   Moon Sign Capricorn*

Decisions you take at the moment tend to be quite lucky, a situation for which you can thank the lunar high. It's time to go for gold and to trust in your own judgement, which tends to be very sound now. Travel could be possible, with holidays beckoning, or trips planned at short notice.

16 TUESDAY ☿ *Moon Age Day 14   Moon Sign Capricorn*

The go-ahead period is still well in operation, and you won't slow down at all today. That means having to push yourself hard, but to do so is certainly not a problem right now. Be prepared to take a few chances. Risks at the moment are very calculated and likely to work out well.

17 WEDNESDAY ☿ *Moon Age Day 15   Moon Sign Capricorn*

Your imagination is well stimulated today by almost everything you see and do. It is very important at the moment not to rush your fences but to take jobs slowly and steadily. That's the way Capricorn works when at its best and it is a sure recipe to greater success, especially in professional matters.

18 THURSDAY ☿ *Moon Age Day 16   Moon Sign Aquarius*

Look out for interesting contacts. Some of these will be people you already know but your life is so much in a state of flux that you are bound to be meeting new people too. Acting on impulse seems attractive from a personal point of view and it is true that you are very disarming right now, so perhaps it is the best policy.

19 FRIDAY ☿ *Moon Age Day 17   Moon Sign Aquarius*

You will almost certainly feel a need for security today, which is why you are making certain that your loved ones are OK and also fishing for declarations of love from your life partner. These feelings are nothing to worry about and are par for the course for presently nervy Capricorn.

20 SATURDAY ☿ *Moon Age Day 18   Moon Sign Pisces*

Upsets in private relationships can distract you in ways far beyond the confines of your own front door, but only if you take them to heart. Emotional upsets now tend to be very fleeting and so it isn't worth hanging on to them for any length of time. Get on with something concrete and you will soon feel happier.

21 SUNDAY ☿ *Moon Age Day 19   Moon Sign Pisces*

It's a good idea right now to check all facts very carefully and to be willing to listen to what those in the know are saying. Although this might mean taking the advice of someone you generally consider to be a rival, you can only gain as a result. Beware that any kind of financial speculation might be a mistake for a few days.

22 MONDAY ☿ *Moon Age Day 20   Moon Sign Pisces*

Trends move on, and there are certain financial matters that now deserve your attention. Some of your plans could be coming to fruition far earlier than you might have expected. This is also a good day for love, with declarations of affection coming from some unlikely or unexpected places so there may be a little confusion regarding your own feelings.

23 TUESDAY ☿ *Moon Age Day 21   Moon Sign Aries*

You need to find a certain amount of time to concentrate on your dreams right now. This doesn't mean sitting around and doing nothing because there is a very strong practical aspect to present trends. It is important is to realise and to accept that there are times when your own wishes are the most important thing in your life.

24 WEDNESDAY ☿ *Moon Age Day 22   Moon Sign Aries*

Your powers of attraction are in the ascendant and so you should not be in the least surprised to find that attention is coming from all manner of directions. In a personal sense this might lead to a slightly embarrassing situation and one that means having to politely tell someone if you are spoken for romantically.

25 THURSDAY   ☿   *Moon Age Day 23*   *Moon Sign Taurus*

You gain by taking a nurturing and supportive role today. Concerns for the needs of family members and even much-cherished friends are likely to crop up regularly and might interfere with the smooth running of your day. Capricorn might also be in an over-nostalgic mood at present.

26 FRIDAY   ☿   *Moon Age Day 24*   *Moon Sign Taurus*

The things you say have a great bearing on the way others behave, so you need to take particular care right now. The slightest encouragement on your part could lead to untold changes taking place, which is fine as long as people know whether you are serious in the advice you are offering.

27 SATURDAY   ☿   *Moon Age Day 25*   *Moon Sign Taurus*

Today looks set to bring love and romance into your life, even if you weren't expecting it. Those you care for the most are now prepared to let you get away with almost anything and it is also clear that the more humorous side of your character is going to be fully on display.

28 SUNDAY   ☿   *Moon Age Day 26*   *Moon Sign Gemini*

It seems you are in a more 'give and take' frame of mind than might sometimes be the case. This could lead to an interesting sort of Sunday and one during which co-operation pays dividends for everyone concerned. If you have been considering throwing in your lot with any sort of group, go right ahead.

29 MONDAY   ☿   *Moon Age Day 27*   *Moon Sign Gemini*

It is important to organise your time efficiently and to be willing to make significant changes if you know they are necessary. This may not please everyone but trying to make your own circumstances fit that of the people around you impossible. Just be kind and explain yourself as much as you can.

30 TUESDAY ☿ *Moon Age Day 28   Moon Sign Cancer*

It's time to recharge flagging batteries, which is just about all you can do whilst the lunar low is around. You can spend time with family members, or perhaps think about a heart-to-heart with your partner. What you don't need at the moment is to put yourself under any unnecessary pressure.

31 WEDNESDAY ☿ *Moon Age Day 0   Moon Sign Cancer*

Content to take a back seat away from the action, you are able to look at matters in a fresh light today. An occasional enforced absence from the mainstream doesn't do you any harm at all. On the contrary, it makes it possible for you to look at routine situations in a revolutionary way.

August 2019

1 THURSDAY
Moon Age Day 1   Moon Sign Leo

You have a great deal of charm today, which might mean that you can be cheeky and get away with all sorts. Don't forget to keep in touch with family members who are at a distance, and also friends you haven't seen for quite some time.

2 FRIDAY
Moon Age Day 2   Moon Sign Leo

Now things are changing and you need to look towards some difference and diversity in your life. After a week or more of feeling generally satisfied to stand still, now you want to move around. Today offers some opportunities to do so and should also bring a good deal in the way of social interaction.

3 SATURDAY
Moon Age Day 3   Moon Sign Virgo

You now enjoy the company of a whole host of different people. Be willing to spend time with them, especially if they have a very different view of life than the one you generally hold. Don't get involved in family rows. You won't be starting them and haven't a great deal to contribute so keep well away.

4 SUNDAY
Moon Age Day 4   Moon Sign Virgo

Prepare for a slightly difficult day emotionally. You need to be absolutely sure that you understand what others are saying, especially your partner. As long as you are willing to talk things through sensibly, then all should be well. What you shouldn't do is fly off the handle without being fully in possession of the facts.

5 MONDAY
Moon Age Day 5   Moon Sign Libra

Today you should be able to bring a professional situation to a satisfactory conclusion and should find that you have a strong edge when dealing with those who have a different strategy. Your confidence is definitely on the increase and is stimulated by the number of people calling upon you for advice.

6 TUESDAY
Moon Age Day 6   Moon Sign Libra

As far as the material world is concerned, you may fail to make the sort of progress you might wish today. Never mind, instead of worrying too much about money, turn your mind in the direction of personal relationships, which can offer a great deal. Because you feel somewhat threatened you might retreat into routines.

7 WEDNESDAY
Moon Age Day 7   Moon Sign Scorpio

Put some ingenious ideas to the test and enlist the help of like-minded people whenever you can today. Don't be afraid to be out on a limb, or to make the most of situations that others think are past their sell-by date. You are an original at present, and won't be afraid to show it.

8 THURSDAY
Moon Age Day 8   Moon Sign Scorpio

Avoid ill-conceived ideas, most of which probably originate with someone else. Don't commit yourself to anything until you have looked closely at the details and are certain of your options. It might be best to stay right away from business of any sort if you can today, because pleasure is now more rewarding.

9 FRIDAY
Moon Age Day 9   Moon Sign Sagittarius

Close emotional attachments work better for you today than casual friendships or even associations at work. It might not be easy to see your way forward, particularly in a financial sense, but there are always people around to offer sound advice and a helping hand.

10 SATURDAY   *Moon Age Day 10   Moon Sign Sagittarius*

Although your mind today might be almost anywhere except on the task at hand, there is a dreamy sort of quality to your thinking that feels very seductive. You can get things done, especially if you enrol the support of people within your family or maybe friends. Subconsciously, you are on the verge of a breakthrough.

11 SUNDAY   *Moon Age Day 11   Moon Sign Sagittarius*

Sunday brings a slight slowing of the pace, though certainly not for long. In a social and personal sense you might not even notice a change of pace. True, you will be pleased to luxuriate somewhat, and you won't take kindly to being overwhelmed with work at the present time.

12 MONDAY   *Moon Age Day 12   Moon Sign Capricorn*

Things change quickly as the lunar high begins to take hold of your life. Any timidity that could have been evident yesterday now disappears altogether, leaving you feeling extra confident and anxious to make a big impression. That shouldn't be difficult, especially in a social sense.

13 TUESDAY   *Moon Age Day 13   Moon Sign Capricorn*

Lady Luck may be behind you today, pointing you in the direction of some significant gains in a number of areas. Look out for love knocking on your door and don't turn away from the chance to show what you can really do. There may be some upheavals in a family sense, but you are not causing them.

14 WEDNESDAY   *Moon Age Day 14   Moon Sign Aquarius*

The beneficial high-energy period is maintained even as the lunar high moves away, as you zip through chores in a quarter of the time they would usually take. Chill out when someone is trying to annoy you, because you won't gain any house points by rising to the bait. It might be best not to get involved in any heated discussions.

15 THURSDAY   *Moon Age Day 15   Moon Sign Aquarius*

You ought to be in a really good position to call the shots in most situations now. The nearer you get to your chosen goals, the better you feel about yourself and life in general. Events taking place outdoors are highlighted this Thursday so you will probably want to get out and enjoy any good weather.

16 FRIDAY   *Moon Age Day 16   Moon Sign Aquarius*

The opportunities for greater freedom have rarely seemed better than they are at present. Many Capricorns will desire a more independent lifestyle, though you will have to curb your insistence and enthusiasm a little if you don't want to upset others on the way. Don't allow little things to upset you.

17 SATURDAY   *Moon Age Day 17   Moon Sign Pisces*

Communication with others may give you a lift today, brought about by a definite change in the way others are listening to your particular point of view. Avoid getting involved in pointless arguments if you are at work and save your more adversarial qualities for another day. Agreement is better than argument now.

18 SUNDAY   *Moon Age Day 18   Moon Sign Pisces*

Strong emotions influence your thinking at present, especially those that are tied to personal attachments. If you don't understand why a particular person is acting in a particular way, there is no reason to remain confused. Simply open your mouth and ask.

19 MONDAY   *Moon Age Day 19   Moon Sign Aries*

Don't spend on impulse today; in fact don't spend at all unless you are certain that the money is going in a sensible direction. You should check all documents carefully before committing to them and ask the advice of a worldly friend regarding any business transaction you don't fully understand.

20 TUESDAY   *Moon Age Day 20   Moon Sign Aries*

There is likely to be a more relaxed feeling generally today. This is partly because professional progress is good and so you may not be worrying about work. In addition, this could be one of the best days of the month for getting away from it all. You may be strongly attracted to a newcomer.

21 WEDNESDAY   *Moon Age Day 21   Moon Sign Aries*

At work you have much energy but are tempering practical efforts with getting to know associates and even superiors better. There may be some gains in the financial sphere, though these are likely to relate to things you did in the past rather than to anything you are doing at present.

22 THURSDAY   *Moon Age Day 22   Moon Sign Taurus*

There are definitely some intellectual challenges around at this stage of the week and you are more than equal to them. Don't choose the most complicated way of doing anything, even though this might appear to be more thorough. Sometimes the easiest way is best, even for the zodiac sign of Capricorn.

23 FRIDAY   *Moon Age Day 23   Moon Sign Taurus*

There is plenty out there in the big, wide world to interest you but you could find that mundane responsibilities are preventing you from sampling it. Don't worry too much about everyday concerns, many of which will still be there tomorrow. Do what is vital at the start of today and then take some hours to yourself.

24 SATURDAY   *Moon Age Day 24   Moon Sign Gemini*

Put the power of your personality to good use as early in the day as you can. This is no time to let matters ride, especially when you know that to act quickly may bring significant gains. Even when others don't agree with your present point of view it might be necessary to move forward in any case.

25 SUNDAY
Moon Age Day 25   Moon Sign Gemini

This is a day on which many of your views may be challenged. The people who have recently been accepting what you had to say without question are now more inclined to interrogate you. This might not always be a comfortable experience but since you have most of the answers, there is no reason to worry unduly.

26 MONDAY
Moon Age Day 26   Moon Sign Cancer

Take some time out to relax and enjoy the peace and quiet that this little island in amongst the busy ocean of life can offer. You will probably be happy to spend a few hours with a good book if you can, especially if you can get out into the fresh air. If you have a garden, you would enjoy spending time there around now.

27 TUESDAY
Moon Age Day 27   Moon Sign Cancer

It may be slightly unwise to believe absolutely everything you hear today, even on those occasions when it seems to be coming from a reliable source. When it comes to getting through tasks you don't care for, simply plough on, though with your mind set on some little treats for later.

28 WEDNESDAY
Moon Age Day 28   Moon Sign Leo

Material considerations are uppermost in your mind and there isn't much doubt you are in the market to enjoy some of the finer things of life. Don't be too quick to judge the considerations or even the actions of family members. You might not know all the details and so would not be a position to fully understand.

29 THURSDAY
Moon Age Day 29   Moon Sign Leo

Perhaps this would not be the best time to be overconfident in your own abilities. A little apparent humility can go a long way, even if it is only to make those around you feel more capable. Underneath any bravado you have a sweet disposition and an overriding desire to please your loved ones. This is quite obvious now.

30 FRIDAY
Moon Age Day 0   Moon Sign Virgo

You like to be in charge and won't have any difficulty at all telling others what to do. Whether or not they take kindly to this present trait depends on the way you handle situations. This is another period that carries an overwhelming desire to try new things and to see places that could be far away.

31 SATURDAY
Moon Age Day 1   Moon Sign Virgo

It is sometimes too easy to become attracted to fantasies, even for a realistic and down-to-earth Capricorn. If you suspect this might be the case, you need to look long and hard at your reasoning right now. Of course there's nothing wrong with make-believe, as long as you know that's what it is.

September
2019

1 SUNDAY
Moon Age Day 2   Moon Sign Libra

You certainly intend to be heard today and you won't be backward when it comes to letting people know what you think. Do your best to make sure you don't give any unintentional offence. The present planetary picture can take just a little of the recent charm out of your nature.

2 MONDAY
Moon Age Day 3   Moon Sign Libra

There are some potentially interesting encounters around during today, though not of course if you insist on staying behind closed doors. Now you need to spread your wings and there are people around you who will be only too willing to take a trip somewhere special with you.

3 TUESDAY
Moon Age Day 4   Moon Sign Scorpio

This would be as good a time as any to take an idea you have had recently and to run with it. With some fairly influential people around, you could ask for endorsements and also make headway, even against the odds. Capricorn is irrepressible at present, perhaps more so than at any other time this year.

4 WEDNESDAY
Moon Age Day 5   Moon Sign Scorpio

You can't please all of the people all of the time, a saying that is likely to make real sense to you today. There are times when it is pointless trying and in the end all you can do is be certain you are doing your best. Some people might disbelieve even that but that's the way life is.

5 THURSDAY
Moon Age Day 6   Moon Sign Scorpio

You are probably making a greater impression on some people than you think. This is especially likely to be the case with those who are your intended romantic targets. Capricorn is not showy or particularly noisy but you can still let people know you are around. Your confidence is almost palpable today.

6 FRIDAY
Moon Age Day 7   Moon Sign Sagittarius

If you refuse to listen to others today, it's possible that you are doing both them and you a definite disfavour. Even people you haven't thought of as being the types to offer advice have some interesting things to say now. On a different note, trends indicate that you need to be sure that letters are posted and emails sent.

7 SATURDAY
Moon Age Day 8   Moon Sign Sagittarius

Where communication is concerned, you have it within you to get the best from others today. You have a natural tendency at present to fight for the underdog but before you do make certain your support is justified in the particular case. There might also be slightly more money around than you expected.

8 SUNDAY
Moon Age Day 9   Moon Sign Capricorn

Today the lunar high really comes into full force, supercharging your nature and making it easy for you to see the way ahead. If you are single and have wanted to ask someone out, this is the time to do it. Those in longer-term relationships should be getting special support from their partners.

9 MONDAY
Moon Age Day 10   Moon Sign Capricorn

Make sure you are in the right place at the right time if you really want situations to pay off now. This isn't at all difficult because your intuition is sparking and telling you where to go and what to do when you get there. It might be suggested that you are virtually flying on automatic pilot today.

10 TUESDAY   *Moon Age Day 11   Moon Sign Aquarius*

This is a time when you will be asserting your independence and making it plain to almost anyone that you want to plough your own furrow. Although you may encounter a little opposition to your plans right now, in the main your obvious determination will resign others to your chosen course of action.

11 WEDNESDAY   *Moon Age Day 12   Moon Sign Aquarius*

You have plenty of opportunity at the moment to simply be yourself. You might think that the real you is not all that interesting or inspirational but it's what others think that counts. Show some caution in business dealings and don't allow anyone to charm you out of your money.

12 THURSDAY   *Moon Age Day 13   Moon Sign Aquarius*

You have certain duties to fulfil and not all of them are equally enjoyable. However, these should not take the edge off your ability to enjoy this day. Although the inclination to travel has been strong within you for some weeks now, today's tendency makes you more inclined to want to stay near to home.

13 FRIDAY   *Moon Age Day 14   Moon Sign Pisces*

Work and practical matters could provide a few frustrations today. The fact is that you can't make things go the way you would wish and that won't please you at all. Your best area of focus today would be towards your social life, which offers far more in the way of enjoyment than employment presently can.

14 SATURDAY   *Moon Age Day 15   Moon Sign Pisces*

There should be strong elements of social fun about at the moment and a feeling that most things are going your way. You may be quite surprised at the present reaction of associates to some of your ideas and it is also possible that those who are in a position to elevate you are viewing you positively.

15 SUNDAY
Moon Age Day 16   Moon Sign Aries

Don't expect to feel completely in charge of any aspect of your life at the moment and this includes personal issues. It looks as though you are going to have to rely on the good offices of family members, especially your partner. Although you may be lacking in practical abilities just now your imagination knows no bounds.

16 MONDAY
Moon Age Day 17   Moon Sign Aries

The more variety you have in your life, the better you are likely to enjoy yourself today. The start of this new working week signals the chance to score significantly more success than was possible last week. Right from the start enlist the support of people you know to have similar ideas to your own.

17 TUESDAY
Moon Age Day 18   Moon Sign Aries

You are now at your best when it comes to working with and dealing with others and you know very well what to do in order to make best use of your present practical skills. Your love life should be looking quite good and it is possible that you will meet someone right now who has some important information to impart.

18 WEDNESDAY
Moon Age Day 19   Moon Sign Taurus

Most of those who are close to you seem to rally to your cause at the moment. This could turn out to be something of a problem because you don't really want others thinking and acting on your behalf right now. Have a little patience and be thankful that you are regarded so highly.

19 THURSDAY
Moon Age Day 20   Moon Sign Taurus

Capricorn now shows its assertive side and you really are in a position to call the shots, and not only with regard to your own life. It appears that others are willing to bow to what they consider to be your superior knowledge and judgement and this fills you with even more confidence than you had before.

131

20 FRIDAY
Moon Age Day 21   Moon Sign Gemini

Your judgement is sound and that means that you have to decide the important issues of life for yourself. Although you receive a great deal of support, it won't help if what others want for you runs contrary to your own will. Try to walk a narrow line between self-choice and an apparent stubborn streak that is sometimes present in Capricorn.

21 SATURDAY
Moon Age Day 22   Moon Sign Gemini

Although the best of the summer is now gone and the nights are drawing in, you could be feeling a great need to break the bounds of the usual and to get far from home. In reality, even a short trip would help to prevent you feeling unsettled over the next few days, so get together with someone you really like and take a journey.

22 SUNDAY
Moon Age Day 23   Moon Sign Gemini

Right now the support system on which you are sometimes obliged to rely is as strong as ever and people are virtually queuing up to do what they can for you. This is only just and fair because across the last few months you have been doing so much for them. Take kindness in the spirit in which it is clearly intended.

23 MONDAY
Moon Age Day 24   Moon Sign Cancer

It might be best to suspend major activities wherever you can, at least until Wednesday. That means giving yourself more spare time, some of which you can spend building broken bridges, particularly in the family. The fact that not everyone is seeing eye to eye at present isn't your fault, but it might feel as if it is.

24 TUESDAY
Moon Age Day 25   Moon Sign Cancer

Today is another slightly quieter day and definitely not one during which you should take any financial risks. Keep it light and steady, no matter what you decide to do. If there are parties going on somewhere in your vicinity, you will want to join in, despite the fact that your social skills seem somewhat diminished at present.

25 WEDNESDAY — *Moon Age Day 26   Moon Sign Leo*

Now your powers of attraction are strong and you may find yourself in the most potentially dynamic part of the month as far as romance is concerned. In more practical issues if you get a good start at the beginning of the day you are likely to find that most issues go your way. It's important not to procrastinate.

26 THURSDAY — *Moon Age Day 27   Moon Sign Leo*

Domestic matters should be going fairly well and it won't be at all hard for you to get even younger family members to toe the Capricorn line. All the same, the demands you make on others are still based on the way you view life, which can seem to be a narrow point of view to more gregarious and less tidy types.

27 FRIDAY — *Moon Age Day 28   Moon Sign Virgo*

You will be outgoing and friendly to almost everyone at the moment and that means you will be in great demand. Social trends look particularly good and the weekend ahead offers much in the way of enjoyment. Don't worry too much about practical issues, some of which will take care of themselves.

28 SATURDAY — *Moon Age Day 0   Moon Sign Virgo*

You will probably find that a little privacy is worth a great deal to you at the moment. As your thoughts turn towards the spiritual side of life, it may become clear to those you mix with in the practical, everyday world that you are taking a mental break today. The dreamy side of your personality is certainly on display.

29 SUNDAY — *Moon Age Day 1   Moon Sign Libra*

Avoid being too confrontational in any situation this Sunday and, if necessary, count to ten before you make any contentious comments. One of the issues that might be causing you a little anger is the thought that someone you care for is being put upon. The chances are, though, that for the moment you must allow them to conduct their own battle.

30 MONDAY

Moon Age Day 2   Moon Sign Libra

For most of the time talks and discussions should go the way you would wish at the start of this week, so much so that you may well be in a position to mediate in someone else's dispute. Concentrate on the task at hand, even though your mind is apt to wander slightly as the day wears on.

October 2019

1 TUESDAY
Moon Age Day 3   Moon Sign Scorpio

Most things that are going on at work ought to suit you pretty well at the moment and there probably won't be a moment to stop and think today. With everything to play for you are keen to get going with new tasks and ought to be showing the world just how competent the average Capricorn can be.

2 WEDNESDAY
Moon Age Day 4   Moon Sign Scorpio

Now you need to clear the path towards new developments that are coming into your life, and even though there is a good deal of hard work necessary it's clear that you are up for it. Even casual conversations can bring important messages so it's important to keep your ears open.

3 THURSDAY
Moon Age Day 5   Moon Sign Sagittarius

Expect some real support at this time because that's what you are likely to be getting. Routines are now easier to deal with and when other people are becoming bored or falling by the wayside, you carry on regardless. The attitude of your partner takes some working out but you have the intuition to handle the situation.

4 FRIDAY
Moon Age Day 6   Moon Sign Sagittarius

You should be able to successfully put across your present opinions to almost anyone who will stay around long enough to listen. There are gains to be made through being in the right place at the right time and you should also discover a distinctly sporting or generally competitive edge that could be useful.

5 SATURDAY
Moon Age Day 7   Moon Sign Capricorn

It's a good idea while the lunar high is around to focus on the main priorities of your life and refuse to be distracted. Your quick thinking may prove to be extremely lucky and there ought to be plenty of people around who are captivated by the natural charm you exude from every pore.

6 SUNDAY
Moon Age Day 8   Moon Sign Capricorn

Things can get better and better for the average Capricorn under present trends and all it takes from you is to give a nudge to a swing that is already in motion. You don't need to start anything from scratch as most of what you need to get ahead is already staring you in the face. It's simply a case of realising the fact.

7 MONDAY
Moon Age Day 9   Moon Sign Capricorn

Good spirits prevail everywhere and the start of a new working week ought to find you filled with enthusiasm and just aching to take control in some way. If you have been waiting for news regarding a family member or close friend, you might have to hang on a little longer but the delay should be worthwhile.

8 TUESDAY
Moon Age Day 10   Moon Sign Aquarius

When it comes to attracting life's little luxuries you are certainly not at the back of the queue right now. You are concentrating on the task at hand but others will deal with issues that are a puzzle to you if you give them the chance. Co-operative ventures can be very rewarding but that means sharing.

9 WEDNESDAY
Moon Age Day 11   Moon Sign Aquarius

A trip out to see friends might be quite gratifying at the moment and you will probably want to make this day your own in some way. Although there is plenty to be done, most of it will still be around tomorrow. For this reason if no other you should take some time out today to simply please yourself, if you can.

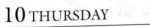

10 THURSDAY
Moon Age Day 12   Moon Sign Pisces

The pace of everyday life is quickened as you respond positively to the many incentives that surround you at this time. Major priorities are emphasised in your chart and there ought to be plenty to keep you occupied. Look out for love because romance is likely to play an important part in your life around now.

11 FRIDAY
Moon Age Day 13   Moon Sign Pisces

There are some distractions around right now and you will need to work hard in order to keep your mind on the task at hand. By the evening the social possibilities are likely to be so good that there is no chance of doing so at all. The suggestion here is to give in and join with others in some sort of happy diversion.

12 SATURDAY
Moon Age Day 14   Moon Sign Pisces

You should have little or no problem getting any material desires this weekend. Don't work harder than you have to and remember that life is about playing too. Luxuries are now quite easy to come by and some of them turn up from fairly unexpected places. Prepare for a friend in need to enlist your aid.

13 SUNDAY
Moon Age Day 15   Moon Sign Aries

Talks and general negotiations are likely to go your way at the moment so it is worth spending time chatting about almost anything. You show the necessary ability to compromise when it matters the most and won't be as stubborn as can sometimes be the case for your zodiac sign. Try for some variety in the evening.

14 MONDAY
Moon Age Day 16   Moon Sign Aries

Something you need to know work-wise or to do with the practical aspects of life is coming your way now, so keep listening. Avoid getting involved in family rows or indeed arguments of any kind. Although you are not likely to be starting them the blame might come your way unless you keep away altogether.

15 TUESDAY
Moon Age Day 17   Moon Sign Taurus

In a financial sense you can expect a few ups and downs at this time. However, you are adapting very well to changing circumstances and should win out in most situations. Don't be too quick to apportion blame when something goes slightly wrong. You might discover that the responsibility is yours.

16 WEDNESDAY
Moon Age Day 18   Moon Sign Taurus

Favourable travel trends are now around and it doesn't matter whether the possibilities are for short-term trips or longer breaks. You need change in your life and will be seeking it wherever you can. This would also be a very good time to brush up your computer skills and to get busy in the internet.

17 THURSDAY
Moon Age Day 19   Moon Sign Taurus

If there are any personal restrictions today, they are likely to annoy you a great deal. The truth is that Capricorn knows where it wants to go and won't take kindly to being prevented from doing so. All the same, you retain the essential popularity that is your usual lot.

18 FRIDAY
Moon Age Day 20   Moon Sign Gemini

This is the time to ditch whatever has been holding you back. If this is going to prove awkward or embarrassing, you might have to think things through first. What you can't do is carry on down a road that definitely isn't the right one for you. Comfort and security mean a great deal by the evening.

19 SATURDAY
Moon Age Day 21   Moon Sign Gemini

Your sense of adventure is strong this Saturday. You almost certainly will not want to stay at home and put your feet up. This is the sort of period during which you set yourself a challenge and then go out and win. Advice from others is well intentioned but you probably don't want it at all.

20 SUNDAY   *Moon Age Day 22   Moon Sign Cancer*

You need to leave just a little room for errors at the moment and probably won't want to be biting off more than you can chew. There's a generally lazy phase on the way for some and a need to rely more heavily on the help and advice that comes from other directions. It's time to call in a few favours.

21 MONDAY   *Moon Age Day 23   Moon Sign Cancer*

There could be minor tensions to be dealt with around now and a few family arguments are possible. The secret is not to get involved if you can avoid doing so at all. Casual conversations give you good ideas for later but for the moment just deal with what you have to and don't push yourself too hard.

22 TUESDAY   *Moon Age Day 24   Moon Sign Leo*

Now it's time to get busy. With energy levels back up to full and a genuine desire to get things done, you will want to make an early start today. Once the practical necessities of the day are sorted, it's time to go out and have fun. You probably won't stop moving from the time you wake up until the moment you go to bed again.

23 WEDNESDAY   *Moon Age Day 25   Moon Sign Leo*

Relationships of almost any sort can be emotionally uplifting but where love and romance are concerned, the world should be your oyster right now. You enjoy plenty of confidence, especially in personal rather than professional situations. You might also be on the receiving end of a very special favour.

24 THURSDAY   *Moon Age Day 26   Moon Sign Virgo*

You can't believe everything you hear today, even if in a few cases you wish you could. A good dose of scepticism proves to be necessary because there are tall tales around. And just when you think everyone is talking nonsense, the silliest story of all might just turn out to be true!

25 FRIDAY
Moon Age Day 27   Moon Sign Virgo

Gaining more in the way of financial resources could be your main priority at present. Although it might seem at first that there is nowhere you can get more cash, that logical and methodical Capricorn approach should win out in the end. In social encounters, you tend to shine now.

26 SATURDAY
Moon Age Day 28   Moon Sign Libra

Important discussions or negotiations can turn up trumps for you today and could lead you to finding a way forward professionally that hasn't been an option before. Talk, talk and more talk is what matters for Capricorn today because that's the only way you are going to alter anything.

27 SUNDAY
Moon Age Day 0   Moon Sign Libra

Because there is much to get done today, certain issues may have to be re-routed or even changed altogether. There can be a feeling of dislocation and a tendency to fight shy of things you don't want to face. If you think it might be helpful, it would be sensible to talk to someone who is in the know.

28 MONDAY
Moon Age Day 1   Moon Sign Scorpio

Happy encounters with people from the past are quite likely to take place at any time now. There is a sense of nostalgia about that is difficult to define, yet which can be of use if you view it positively. One thing is certain – don't dwell on the past because that could lead to unfair comparisons in your mind.

29 TUESDAY
Moon Age Day 2   Moon Sign Scorpio

Getting what you want, either in a professional or a personal sense, should not be at all difficult now. You have strong willpower and a determination that cannot be bettered by any other zodiac sign. Decide what you want from life and find some unique ways to go about getting it.

30 WEDNESDAY   *Moon Age Day 3   Moon Sign Sagittarius*

A long-standing commitment needs to be addressed as October draws to an end. Get it out of the way as quickly as you can because what matters is leaving yourself free to do the things that come upon you quickly. Negotiating your path through a pile of red tape might not help but you are equal enough to the task.

31 THURSDAY   *Moon Age Day 4   Moon Sign Sagittarius*

You may feel as though travel plans are something you want to think about today. If you have any journey planned in the very near future, make sure that you have all the details sorted. Small disagreements with your partner or family members should not be taken out of proportion.

November 2019

1 FRIDAY
☿ *Moon Age Day 5   Moon Sign Sagittarius*

This would be a good time to get practical work out of the way, something that is quite easy for Capricorn under almost any circumstances. It's just possible that the critical attitude of work-mates is either upsetting you or slowing down your pace somewhat. Remember that you don't have to take any notice of them.

2 SATURDAY
☿ *Moon Age Day 6   Moon Sign Capricorn*

With the lunar high comes a sudden burst of enthusiasm and energy. It's as if you have a rocket strapped to your back, so getting through any number of jobs should be a piece of cake. This would be an ideal time to take a journey, preferably in the company of your partner or a good friend.

3 SUNDAY
☿ *Moon Age Day 7   Moon Sign Capricorn*

There is no letup in the pace, despite the arrival of Sunday. You want to be everywhere at the same time and won't take kindly to being held back by anyone. Your confidence is high and so is your popularity. If there is something you particularly want at this stage, you will have the courage to ask for it.

4 MONDAY
☿ *Moon Age Day 8   Moon Sign Aquarius*

Things could be slightly sluggish in a professional sense, so it would be best to only do what you have to at work. Domestically speaking, life should be rather easier to address and in truth, you will be happiest today when at home. You might relish the prospect of simply putting your feet up.

5 TUESDAY ☿ *Moon Age Day 9   Moon Sign Aquarius*

Friends could turn out to be quite helpful, perhaps in fairly unexpected ways. Don't be too proud to accept their assistance, even though in at least some cases you could manage better on your own. Keep a sense of proportion when dealing with issues that have stumped you in the past. Persistence pays off in the end.

6 WEDNESDAY ☿ *Moon Age Day 10   Moon Sign Pisces*

Events in your life run so quickly it might be hard to keep up with them. Comfort and security seem extremely important to you at the present time, which is one of the reasons you find it hard to motivate yourself. By tomorrow your energy levels will be much higher.

7 THURSDAY ☿ *Moon Age Day 11   Moon Sign Pisces*

Today you find a positive emphasis being placed on material considerations. That's the sort of month November is turning out to be for you and you take great delight in new possessions. However, make sure that you don't forget that Christmas isn't far away before you spend all your available money.

8 FRIDAY ☿ *Moon Age Day 12   Moon Sign Pisces*

Your mind works swiftly, leading you to arrive at some quite staggering conclusions, often on the spur of the moment. The end of the working week makes specific demands of you, most likely at work. You may be quite pleased to lay down some responsibilities by the evening.

9 SATURDAY ☿ *Moon Age Day 13   Moon Sign Aries*

Getting your own way in financial matters could be surprisingly easy, probably leading you to being rather suspicious about others. Being paranoid on occasions is part of the Capricorn nature, though it is probably unwarranted right now. Create some space to spend a few hours on your own.

10 SUNDAY ☿ *Moon Age Day 14   Moon Sign Aries*

Today you are struck by a burning need for luxury of one sort or another. Capricorn can sometimes be insecure and owning new things feeds your self-esteem. Of course, they aren't really necessary but as long as you don't break the family bank, you can probably afford to indulge yourself a little.

11 MONDAY ☿ *Moon Age Day 15   Moon Sign Taurus*

It may be easier to get what you want from life now, but typical of your nature, you probably won't want it any more. It's the simpler things in life that appeal most at present, for example the company of good friends and being able to enjoy a well-cooked meal. Social trends are good.

12 TUESDAY ☿ *Moon Age Day 16   Moon Sign Taurus*

Close family encounters work well at this time and you could find yourself heavily involved in plans for next month. There are potential gains to be made, especially if you keep your eyes open, so this would be a good time to go shopping. Don't be too quick to pass judgement on the actions of an associate or acquaintance.

13 WEDNESDAY ☿ *Moon Age Day 17   Moon Sign Taurus*

The speed of life increases and it is obvious that you are trying to keep up with matters that are beyond your capability to control. Seek out the advice and perhaps the help of people who are experts in their respective fields. Even Capricorn cannot do everything for itself, despite the desire to do so.

14 THURSDAY ☿ *Moon Age Day 18   Moon Sign Gemini*

Look out for a period of probable professional gain, mainly brought about as a result of your own attitude and hard work. Some confusion in your social life could arise, as you try to do a dozen different things at the same time. Prepare for some surprising and very interesting news later in the day.

15 FRIDAY ☿ *Moon Age Day 19 Moon Sign Gemini*

The domestic atmosphere is likely to become livelier, with much communication taking place and a possible visit from relatives or friends on the cards. You can expect a number of surprises and unbidden events, all of which contribute to a general increase in interest and participation on your part.

16 SATURDAY ☿ *Moon Age Day 20 Moon Sign Cancer*

It would be best to keep a low profile today, especially if you work at the weekend. Allow others to make the running, whilst you sit and think about the direction you want to take eventually. There is a dreamy side to your nature and you can thank the Moon in Cancer for that tendency.

17 SUNDAY ☿ *Moon Age Day 21 Moon Sign Cancer*

A few obstacles could prevent you from making quite as much of this Sunday as you would wish. However, if you set your stall out carefully, you should be able to get away with barely noticing the lunar low. This would not be a good day to climb a mountain or to take part in other vigorous exercise.

18 MONDAY ☿ *Moon Age Day 22 Moon Sign Leo*

Beware of something of a hitch arising in a practical matter. This will need your attention and capabilities, so don't consider leaving it to anyone else. You are very generous and kind-hearted right now but it is possible you see certain others as being slightly more capable than they actually are.

19 TUESDAY ☿ *Moon Age Day 23 Moon Sign Leo*

Your love life is now characterised by a sense of harmony and a willingness to put yourself out for your partner or sweetheart. Social matters follow a similar pattern and your level of popularity increases apace as you show a warm and caring attitude generally. You may be able to sort out the problems of a friend single-handedly.

20 WEDNESDAY ☿   *Moon Age Day 24   Moon Sign Leo*

The conversations you have with others at this time tend to be pleasant and sympathetic in both directions. Visits to family members or even friends you don't see very often might prove to be very rewarding and you seem to be in a particularly social frame of mind during the middle of this week.

21 THURSDAY   *Moon Age Day 25   Moon Sign Virgo*

Generally speaking you should be feeling relaxed and easy-going right now. There could be a certain something missing from your life, even though it will be hard to work out what this might be. Your love life could well prove to be the most interesting and productive sphere today.

22 FRIDAY   *Moon Age Day 26   Moon Sign Virgo*

At home you have empathy and understanding by the bucket load, but the same cannot be said to be the case out there in the big, wide world. On the contrary, you might display a slightly ruthless attitude in certain situations. Of course you have to guard yourself against tricksters but make sure you are not going too far.

23 SATURDAY   *Moon Age Day 27   Moon Sign Libra*

This is now a period when your ego and determination appear to have reached a peak. Throughout the whole of November you won't be more certain of your position in life than now but you need to exercise some care because one or two issues are not quite what they seem. Once again you seem to be pushing a little too hard.

24 SUNDAY   *Moon Age Day 28   Moon Sign Libra*

Take the opportunity to improve aspects of your domestic life by using your imagination now. In particular, you gain from better romantic trends and should now be showing a far more understanding, comforting and soft quality, something that may have been distinctly lacking for a few days.

25 MONDAY   *Moon Age Day 29   Moon Sign Scorpio*

Try to make this a special day for yourself and your nearest and dearest by dealing with practical matters and by making the sort of progress that might have been difficult a week or two ago. It is clear that you have everything you need to make the most favourable of impressions when it really counts.

26 TUESDAY   *Moon Age Day 0   Moon Sign Scorpio*

The assistance of others cannot be overstated right now, no matter what you decide to do. It's late in the year for travel but you definitely have a desire to get out and about as much as you can. The diplomatic qualities of your nature are also really on display and you make a good arbitrator.

27 WEDNESDAY   *Moon Age Day 1   Moon Sign Sagittarius*

Your social life expands and the middle of this week is the best time for getting together in groups. These trends are also good professionally so you should not be surprised to find that you are being singled out for greater responsibilities. Almost everyone you meet has a unique and interesting point of view.

28 THURSDAY   *Moon Age Day 2   Moon Sign Sagittarius*

You may take a different and more stimulating approach in discussions at work, even if those at home seem to be somehow 'sugar coated' at the moment. It is in a professional sense that the competitive qualities of your nature are on display. You need this hard edge on occasion but it's impossible domestically right now.

29 FRIDAY   *Moon Age Day 3   Moon Sign Capricorn*

The lunar high arrives at a time when quite a few astrological trends are turning in your favour. You can expect the best from what life has to offer but much of what pleases you is as a direct result of your own efforts. There are particularly good financial trends surrounding you.

30 SATURDAY　　　*Moon Age Day 4　Moon Sign Capricorn*

If you are prepared to work just a little harder, almost anything you desire can come your way. The start of the weekend for many marks a time when material and social trends achieve a good balance. People tend to be helpful, even without trying. Much romantic attention is also coming your way.

December

2019

1 SUNDAY
Moon Age Day 5   Moon Sign Aquarius

Today you tend to be happy and emotionally optimistic. Your positive frame of mind is an inspiration to just about anyone you meet, making this a good time for romance or simply for mixing and mingling with people generally. What most people recognise is your finesse and charm.

2 MONDAY
Moon Age Day 6   Moon Sign Aquarius

Though career matters might have rather less going for them than has been the case lately, you should certainly be enjoying yourself in terms of your personal life. Compliments are easy to come by and you are likely to turn heads wherever you go, especially by the evening.

3 TUESDAY
Moon Age Day 7   Moon Sign Aquarius

Financially speaking, you could benefit from some minor improvements now, and not a moment too soon with Christmas so close. Nevertheless, you need to spend wisely and to look out for those bargains that are around every corner. All in all, this could be one of the best days of December for shopping.

4 WEDNESDAY
Moon Age Day 8   Moon Sign Pisces

Personal and intimate matters are the most rewarding of all this Wednesday. You will be quite busy as you go about your day, but you should set aside some time to show your partner how much you care. The response you get will be very positive and should see you finishing the day on a high note.

5 THURSDAY
Moon Age Day 9   Moon Sign Pisces

You could easily get the feeling that you are speaking out of turn today. That's fine, but unless you say what you think, how on earth will others know? It's really a case of 'speak the truth and shame the devil', just as long as you remember to use a little tact on the way.

6 FRIDAY
Moon Age Day 10   Moon Sign Aries

The time is right to establish good relations with just about anyone, even people who have not been your favourites in the past. There is a good chance that you are being taken more seriously now and that you might attract, as a friend, someone who was never very kind to you in years gone by.

7 SATURDAY
Moon Age Day 11   Moon Sign Aries

Although today starts out fairly steadily, things should soon heat up. Progress is hard to see at first, which is why by lunchtime, you have to put in that extra bit of effort that can make all the difference. By the evening, you can be the life and soul of any party. If there isn't one on offer, you might throw one yourself.

8 SUNDAY
Moon Age Day 12   Moon Sign Aries

A sense that you can rely only on yourself might prevail today. Up to a point that might be the case, but you ought to give friends the benefit of the doubt all the same. Offer others a helping hand in specific tasks that are familiar to you but don't get in the way if younger people are seeking independence.

9 MONDAY
Moon Age Day 13   Moon Sign Taurus

You could feel in quite a hurry to complete a particular project today and anxious not to allow anything to get in your way. In all probability this might be something you should have done days or weeks ago, but trends don't suggest that this is now the right time to address it. Put it on the shelf until later.

10 TUESDAY   *Moon Age Day 14   Moon Sign Taurus*

Your love life is well highlighted today, as is travel, perhaps to see people you haven't shared an hour or two with for quite a long time. Although you might be bullied into doing things that go against the grain, the turn of events could surprise you in the end. It is worth putting yourself out.

11 WEDNESDAY   *Moon Age Day 15   Moon Sign Gemini*

Communications are highlighted in your chart today. Make sure that you get any message across to the intended recipient intact. Don't be too willing to judge others for merely doing things you have done yourself in the past. It would be sensible to take a sympathetic point of view whenever possible today.

12 THURSDAY   *Moon Age Day 16   Moon Sign Gemini*

It isn't difficult for you to maintain a high profile in most situations at this stage of the working week. Many Capricorns will be putting thoughts of Christmas on hold, opting instead for the chance to get ahead in a professional sense. People really do want to hear what you are saying at present.

13 FRIDAY   *Moon Age Day 17   Moon Sign Cancer*

Now you really will want to quieten things down. The Moon is in your opposite sign, offering moments for reflection. There is certainly something positive about getting this phase out of the way well ahead of the holiday period, and in any case, you can come up with some excellent ideas while you sit thinking.

14 SATURDAY   *Moon Age Day 18   Moon Sign Cancer*

Whatever you decide to take on board today, do bear in mind that your energy is limited and that your recovery rate is not what it might normally be. Because of this, restrict your activities just a little, whilst at the same time making yourself fully conversant with what is happening around you.

15 SUNDAY
Moon Age Day 19   Moon Sign Cancer

Expect a few bonuses now, not least on the romantic front. It appears that you have all the charm you could possibly need at present, so much so that you can get people to do almost anything for you. Don't milk the situation though because you might be found out later on.

16 MONDAY
Moon Age Day 20   Moon Sign Leo

Beneficial domestic circumstances are indicated, though in terms of your career there could be certain issues that need rethinking carefully. It is quite possible that in one or two cases you will have to return to the drawing board and the arrival of the new week makes this complete rethink possible for most Capricorns.

17 TUESDAY
Moon Age Day 21   Moon Sign Leo

You want to find time to seek out new situations and a change of pace but this might not be easy with the holidays so close. The practical necessities of the season will be having a bearing on your behaviour and this can make sweeping changes less than likely.

18 WEDNESDAY
Moon Age Day 22   Moon Sign Virgo

There is a very matter-of-fact element to Capricorn thinking at this time. You can get the most from your career, whilst at the same time committing yourself to new social projects or situations that require your caring side to show. What is most evident right now is your adaptability.

19 THURSDAY
Moon Age Day 23   Moon Sign Virgo

You are a much happier team player at present than would often be the case. Capricorn has not only a pronounced stubborn streak but also an in-built desire to go it alone on occasion. Neither of these traits are showing at present and it is your natural desire to agree with those around you that gets you noticed and which raises your popularity.

20 FRIDAY
Moon Age Day 24   Moon Sign Libra

A little soul searching might be required at the end of this working week. This is a time of increased selflessness and a commitment towards others that is much greater than of late. Maybe you feel that someone has a special need of you right now or it could simply be that your intuition and empathy are running at a high pitch.

21 SATURDAY
Moon Age Day 25   Moon Sign Libra

It could be the home-based side of Christmas that appeals to you the most this time around, though you are chatty, carefree and very good company in any situation. There might be presents of a very singular sort coming your way, one or two of them from a most unexpected direction.

22 SUNDAY
Moon Age Day 26   Moon Sign Scorpio

You may have a slight tendency right now to gloss over something that is actually quite important. It isn't like you to pretend that things are different than they are but that's what appears to be happening for the moment. Try to focus on the big picture and not be to be diverted by the excitement and glitter of the season.

23 MONDAY
Moon Age Day 27   Moon Sign Scorpio

A word in the right ear can work near miracles at the moment and your general level of luck is high. A little measured, cautious speculation might be in order. At work it's clear that you know exactly what is expected of you and how best to move forward. In a way this is a pity because there is likely to an enforced break ahead.

24 TUESDAY
Moon Age Day 28   Moon Sign Sagittarius

Christmas Eve finds you quite willing to speak your mind, arguably to a degree that isn't very sensible. Some of the consequences of maintaining such a high profile are not especially what you would wish though it is clear you are willing to take the rough with the smooth. By the evening you should be quite relaxed.

25 WEDNESDAY *Moon Age Day 29   Moon Sign Sagittarius*

Most of the planetary influences that stand around you today are fairly neutral, so whether this turns out to be an excellent Christmas Day is down to your own attitude. You love to talk at the moment and will be getting on very well with most people – even those you don't generally care for all that much.

26 THURSDAY *Moon Age Day 0   Moon Sign Capricorn*

You may be in for the best – and longest – Boxing Day bash you have known for years. Today and tomorrow coincide with the lunar high, bringing a fun-filled attitude, together with an instinctive understanding of how to keep people laughing. Almost anything you do today is tinged with genius.

27 FRIDAY *Moon Age Day 1   Moon Sign Capricorn*

Your enthusiasm remains at a peak and this is certainly no bad way to continue the holidays. All you are really interested in today is having fun, together with making it possible for those around you to have a good time too. There is plenty of scope for romance, too, as you may find out.

28 SATURDAY *Moon Age Day 2   Moon Sign Capricorn*

Your curiosity is very well highlighted today, which is why you won't take any situation for granted but want to know why it has come about. Family times are well accented but so is travel and that could mean jumping in the car or on a bus in order to go and see someone.

29 SUNDAY *Moon Age Day 3   Moon Sign Aquarius*

There are jobs to do today that you don't like the look of and there isn't really much you can do except to pitch in and get on with them. Someone you don't see very often could be making a return visit to your life. If this is a past romantic partner there might be a little embarrassment involved.

30 MONDAY   *Moon Age Day 4   Moon Sign Aquarius*

This should be a day during which being at home is not only pleasant but also enlightening and inspirational. Whether or not this has something to do with family members and their attitude remains to be seen. Certainly you can gain from listening to what your partner and relatives have to say.

31 TUESDAY   *Moon Age Day 5   Moon Sign Pisces*

It appears that you will delight in romantic encounters today or in any situation that allows you to please the people you meet. The very best qualities of Capricorn are on display on this New Year's Eve, and almost everyone notices what a charming and warm person you can be. A party tonight would really please you.

RISING SIGNS FOR CAPRICORN

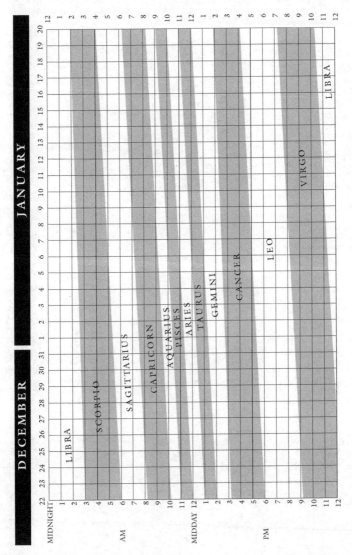

THE ZODIAC, PLANETS AND CORRESPONDENCES

The Earth revolves around the Sun once every calendar year, so when viewed from Earth the Sun appears in a different part of the sky as the year progresses. In astrology, these parts of the sky are divided into the signs of the zodiac and this means that the signs are organised in a circle. The circle begins with Aries and ends with Pisces.

Taking the zodiac sign as a starting point, astrologers then work with all the positions of planets, stars and many other factors to calculate horoscopes and birth charts and tell us what the stars have in store for us.

The table below shows the planets and Elements for each of the signs of the zodiac. Each sign belongs to one of the four Elements: Fire, Air, Earth or Water. Fire signs are creative and enthusiastic; Air signs are mentally active and thoughtful; Earth signs are constructive and practical; Water signs are emotional and have strong feelings.

It also shows the metals and gemstones associated with, or corresponding with, each sign. The correspondence is made when a metal or stone possesses properties that are held in common with a particular sign of the zodiac.

Finally, the table shows the opposite of each star sign – this is the opposite sign in the astrological circle.

Placed	Sign	Symbol	Element	Planet	Metal	Stone	Opposite
1	Aries	Ram	Fire	Mars	Iron	Bloodstone	Libra
2	Taurus	Bull	Earth	Venus	Copper	Sapphire	Scorpio
3	Gemini	Twins	Air	Mercury	Mercury	Tiger's Eye	Sagittarius
4	Cancer	Crab	Water	Moon	Silver	Pearl	Capricorn
5	Leo	Lion	Fire	Sun	Gold	Ruby	Aquarius
6	Virgo	Maiden	Earth	Mercury	Mercury	Sardonyx	Pisces
7	Libra	Scales	Air	Venus	Copper	Sapphire	Aries
8	Scorpio	Scorpion	Water	Pluto	Plutonium	Jasper	Taurus
9	Sagittarius	Archer	Fire	Jupiter	Tin	Topaz	Gemini
10	Capricorn	Goat	Earth	Saturn	Lead	Black Onyx	Cancer
11	Aquarius	Waterbearer	Air	Uranus	Uranium	Amethyst	Leo
12	Pisces	Fishes	Water	Neptune	Tin	Moonstone	Virgo